Succeeding at Life!

Living a Sane, Stable, and Spiritual Life

A realistic approach to discovering how to make your life work for you!

By
Dr. Norman R. Wise

Preface

This was written because there are many hurting and unfulfilled people. Western society has succeeded at producing more wealth and abundance than any society on earth and yet, it has not resulted in producing a sense in most people that they are "succeeding" at life. We find our lives fragmented and divided. There is little harmony or peace in most of our lives. Most of us know behind all of our outward activity there is a quiet desperation. Inwardly, we feel the most critical aspects of our lives are in danger of being neglected or even lost.

This book was written by a Christian pastor, pastoral counselor, life coach and spiritual director. I believe in a Christian worldview. I understand that you may believe in another worldview. I attempted to write this book so that even if you do not believe in my view of the world, you can still benefit from it. Regardless of our various perspectives, we all share the same universe. The truth is "gravity works" whatever your belief system. All of us do have some common ground found in reality and are governed by some common life principles.

If you are coming from a worldview that is not Christian, I am asking you to trust I will treat you with respect in this book. It can be valuable having dialogue with people even when they come from a different perspective. There is value in having a "civil discourse" with those we differ with about life. This is a lot to ask, but I hope you will consider it. It is my deepest desire for you to gain from the truths in this book, even though we disagree about Jesus Christ.

I wish I could say because one formally approaches life from a Christian worldview or has an experience defined as "born again" this leads to succeeding at life. We all know this is not the case. Christians, just as people who follow other worldviews, find their lives filled with disharmony and lack of fulfillment. All of us value finding inner contentment and relational harmony. Yet, few of us do. Every human being, regardless of their worldview can sense when they are losing at life.

While I believe there are great advantages to the Christian worldview (which is obvious since I am committed to it), simply holding to this perspective while ignoring the God-given life principles of reality will not eliminate futility, frustration, or unfruitful endeavors. Those outside the Christian worldview sometimes think we are saying if you go through one dynamic experience with God, all becomes right with your life. At times, this seems to be the message the popular Christian media presents on television. However, the reality is Jesus said "follow me" and was talking about a lifestyle of transforming faith, not a momentary religious high as the road to succeeding at life.

I believe the life principles we find in creation are consistent with a Christian world and life view. These principles are applications of truths imbedded into the very fiber of reality. I believe they were imbedded by the Creator God for the good of all human beings living on this planet. Once we deeply comprehend these divine patterns of life and adapt ourselves to them, we begin finding life fulfillment and healthy pleasure. In this temporal sense, all of God's creation will be blessed by conforming themselves to the realities He has placed in them and in the world in which they live (see Psalm 145).

1

I hope you will now join me on this journey. We will search together for the succeeding principles of life. How could any of us doubt seeking a better understanding of these concepts may help us succeed at life more often? How can this not be worth the quest? I am honored by your willingness to experiment with these concepts. I ask you to open yourself to them. Let us begin.

Introduction: The Forest View of Finding Success

Wholeness is the state of being complete, entire, and balanced with unity among all the parts of our daily living.

Wholeness is a comprehensive experience of healthy effectiveness in our inner being.

Wholeness is a sense of ...

Experiencing a healthy and secure life
Experiencing love for others and being loved
Experiencing healthy laughter
Experiencing learning about reality
Experiencing leaving a good legacy.

To the degree we have these qualities we are whole and succeeding at life.

MAIN PURPOSE OF THIS CHAPTER:

The purpose of this chapter is to give a clear outline of the teaching on how to live a sane, stable, and spiritual life. The hope is to provide a "big picture" on how this book can equip you to succeed at life.

OPENING EXERCISE:

Imagine yourself three years in the future. See yourself mentally, emotionally, psychologically, and spiritually in the most ideal state you can imagine. See some reporter interviewing you and asking about how you came to experiences this transformation over the last three years. What do you tell that reporter? As you imagine yourself in this ideal state of being, do you desire to actually experience it? Does it motivate you to move from your current condition toward your preferred future?

THOUGHTS ON THIS EXERCISE:

_____

_____

_____

_____

_____

AT THIS POINT, YOU MAY BE ASKING YOURSELF ....

You want me to read another book? Are you kidding me? Do I really look like I need another "self help" book to put on my shelf and become another source of frustration, since everything remains the same? Why do you lure me with the temptation to believe there are real answers to life? It is easier to accept the best I can do is to survive not thrive!

I can understand many of you may be thinking some of those things. Obviously there is enough hope and curiosity in you to get to this page, but you may be looking for an excuse to put this book down and justify your view there are no answers to life. There is a sad and sick security in depression and defeat. Giving up before you start can save you a lot of energy. It justifies your apathy.

For those of you, who find yourself in that place; let me encourage you to

believe.

Believe what?

I want you to believe that if you can

➢ get the right perspective;

➢ gain the strength to make wise commitments; and

➢ master the use of effective methodologies; then :

YOU CAN SUCCEED AT LIFE

<u>Why choose to believe this idea?</u>

Because rejecting this idea offers:

- What you have now and what you have had in the past

- Anger for not having answers

- Bitterness over losing

- Despair over never succeeding.

Rejecting the idea that you can succeed gives you lack of hope that the future can be better than the past. Unbelief you can succeed is the root of the anger you feel for life not having purpose. Skepticism that you are able to succeed leads to bitterness over feeling that life is a losing proposition. Doubt you are able to succeed leads eventually to despair over never succeeding and therefore lacking energy to do our best.

So the first step at succeeding at life is to believe that one can

succeed at life

Belief in there being answers to life offers a hopeful future. Faith in being able to learn and practice wise methodologies can give us hope in understanding why our past efforts failed. Confidence in finding solutions offers us the joy of finding answers to life's questions. Trust in there being a way to succeed at life can give us hope of experiencing increasing success in our life. Hope in there being a path that leads to succeeding can give us a new sense of purpose and energy as we face life's challenges. Faith has a lot to offer.

Thoughts about belief

What possible good can come from not taking this journey?

If you are willing to experiment with the "succeeding at life" process, you can find out for yourself if these tools will be effective in helping you reach a state of inner harmony, emotional health, and substantial happiness. If this does not work you are left only where you would have ended if you decided to not experiment with these ideas. You have really lost nothing.

You may be wondering where these principles originate. It is my belief these principles reflect divine wisdom revealed in creation and in the words of Scripture. That would be debated by some. What is for certain is these principles have been developed over thirty years and placed into practice for over a decade at Living Water Life Coaching[1] in Plantation, Florida. These principles have practically helped those who practiced them through the training and mentoring provided by Living Water.

Living Water Life Coaching provides personal mentoring, seminars, and small groups. The approach you will encounter by reading this book was tested in thousands of lives. Where this realistic perspective was adopted, committed to, and applied through wise methodologies, the principles worked!

Here are just a few of the hundreds of testimonies of how effective this approach can be when trusted and applied:

> "My husband and I were on the verge of divorce. It seemed hopeless. We came to Living Water more out of a desire to make our family happy and prove we had 'tried everything' rather than because either of us believed it could work. It is hard to even

---

[1] Living Water Life Coaching was originally called Living Water Counseling.

6

believe that was where we were at. Today, we have not only overcome all the past baggage, but have been trained with tools that help us have a great present with real optimism for our future. This stuff works!" [2]

"Life did not make sense. I felt that things were spinning out of control, but what I have learned from Living Water has allowed me to take joy in my life."

"Living Water helped our family to understand the dynamics of why we could not escape the cycle of insanity. As we used the tools they gave us things have improved and are better than we could have ever hoped."

So I am not asking you to have blind faith. I am asking you to experiment with these principles. I am asking you to consider being trained with a perspective that works. I am asking you to consider committing and engaging this proven effective methodology into your life. It has brought outstanding results in the lives of other people just like you. Why not experiment with it and see if it can help you?

NOTES

_____

_____

_____

_____

_____

_____

_____

_____

_____

---

[2] All the testimonies and illustrations in this book come from the lives of real people who have been helped. Most of them have been part group of people helped by Living Water Life Coaching.

WHAT IS THIS BOOK ABOUT?

The focus of this book is teaching the principles and process necessary to succeed at life.

To succeed at life we must be becoming more and more

sane, stable, and spiritual

- ➤ **Sanity** is understanding what is real.
- ➤ **Stability** is holding on to the truth of what is real regardless of our changing circumstances. It is a commitment to not abandon reality when things get difficult and painful.
- ➤ **Spirituality** is adapting our daily lives to what is eternally real. It is my belief that this eternal reality is best seen in the person and teaching of Jesus of Nazareth who I believe is the Messiah of God.

To succeed at life is to be sane, stable, and spiritual. This is the central message and key truth that must be accepted to succeed at life.

To effectively experience sanity, stability, and spirituality we must relate them to five key areas or spheres of reality. These five spheres are

1. The Proactive Perspective

2. Past Wounds

3. Present Reality

4. Preferred Future

5. Defining Your Life Priorities

Only to the degree we experience sanity, stability, and spirituality in each of these spheres will we succeed at life.

Notes

The following charts outline the book and show how it relates
to these five spheres

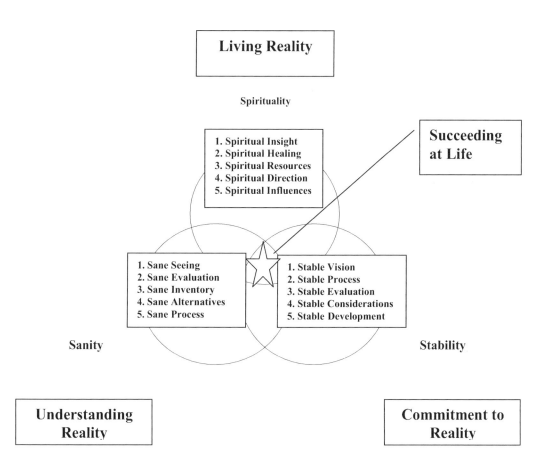

Living Reality

Spirituality

1. Spiritual Insight
2. Spiritual Healing
3. Spiritual Resources
4. Spiritual Direction
5. Spiritual Influences

Succeeding
at Life

1. Sane Seeing
2. Sane Evaluation
3. Sane Inventory
4. Sane Alternatives
5. Sane Process

1. Stable Vision
2. Stable Process
3. Stable Evaluation
4. Stable Considerations
5. Stable Development

Sanity

Stability

Understanding
Reality

Commitment to
Reality

Circle the topics that you feel the most curiosity about.

Ultimately, our aim is to actively be in the process of becoming more and
more sane, stable, and spiritual. Discovering the vision, dedication, and

methods that produce this state in our heart is to find wholeness, inner peace, and succeed at life.[3]

The purpose of sharing this overview is to show you what we will be seeking to experience. The aim is to increase your curiosity and open your heart to the reality that succeeding at life is possible. By seeing this broad picture, it also prepares your mind to begin processing this information and makes it easier for you to remember and apply it. At this point it may seem overwhelming but we will look at each part slowly and carefully. By the end you will have mastered this process and know how to use it.

THE VISION OF THIS BOOK!

The vision of this book is not to just inform you but transform you! The dream of this book is to provide you an effective tool to take you on a journey of self-discovery and self-training in skills of effective living. Therefore, there will be an attempt to not just give your mind information but also your heart inspiration. There will be repetition, so that you can master concepts. In addition, at the end of each chapter there will be exercises and a journal page which will help you apply what is being discussed in the reality of your life. This book is transformational in intention. I ask you to make that your intention as well, as you read these pages and seek to apply them to your life. Don't just read this book but do the recommended exercises. These exercises can and will transform your life.

We are beginning an expedition to discover the principles that can equip us to succeed at life. While you may be plagued with doubts, there is good reason to press forward and engage the truths found within these pages. Take up the challenge and begin this quest for succeeding at life.

My Notes on the introduction:

---

[3]   This book will only deal with the dynamics of becoming a sane, stable, and spiritual mature adult. I plan to write another book which will deal with the principles by which we can have successful relationships.

Exercises for the Introduction

1. When you imagined yourself in the ideal mental, emotional, psychological, and spiritual, future what were the main differences between your ideal perception of yourself and your current perception of yourself?

_____

_____

_____

_____

2. Why do you think some people would be inclined not to believe this material could help them? How would you overcome these objections?

_____

_____

_____

_____

3. What is the greatest thing you could imagine gaining from this material?

_____

_____

_____

Journal Page for the Introduction:

What thoughts and feelings are you having after reading this chapter?

_____

_____

_____

_____

_____

_____

_____

_____

_____

_____

_____

_____

_____

_____

_____

_____

_____

Section One: The Path to Succeeding at Life

Ponder the path of your feet; then all your ways will be sure.

ESV Proverbs 4:26

Chapter One: A Proactive Perspective

The proactive perspective is the belief that we are able to respond to life and take practical actions to improve our state of being. To be proactive is to take 100% responsibility for my thoughts, actions, words, and attitudes. Proactive people show a willingness to confess when they do wrong and feel able to strive to correct it by doing right. This outlook rejects the idea of our thoughts, words, actions, and attitudes have to be the involuntary responses caused by people or circumstances outside of us. [4]

MAIN PURPOSE OF THIS CHAPTER:

To develop an attitude in which we have a framework of life that sees our thoughts, words, and attitudes not flowing to us from the outside so that we are controlled by our environment, but rather we must choose to either accept or reject what culture, family, friends, and circumstances encourage us to become. In this section, you will be challenged to expand that place in your inner life that exists between cause and effect so you can learn to develop, the ability to control yourself regardless of circumstances or the actions of others. This is your ultimate freedom. The freedom of "self determination" is the only real liberty you have. [5]

---

[4] It is admitted that there can be biological factors that influence us. This is still inside of us even though it is not under our control. We can however choose to seek medical help to bring chemical balance to our bodies. While not rejecting the influence of our social environment the perspective rejects the idea that the social environment determines who we are or predestines us towards any particular actions.

[5] It is my belief that the ability of gaining self determination, self control or self management is possible only because of God's grace and mercy working in us. This is one of the gifts of God. There are also good scientific reasons to believe that we have this ability. See the article QUANTUM PHYSICS IN NEUROSCIENCE AND PSYCHOLOGY: A

OPENING EXERCISE:

Imagine driving down the highway and suddenly being cut off by a speeding truck. You have two passengers with you. One of them is Adolph Hitler and the other is Mother Teresa. Does the action of the truck force the two passengers to respond in the same way? How do you imagine Adolph Hitler responding? How to you imagine Mother Teresa responding? What makes the difference in their response?

WHY IS THIS SO HARD TO ACCEPT?

The proactive principle is simple in theory. The proactive principle would teach that people don't make me angry; I choose to respond in an angry way to what they do. At times an angry response may be proper and appropriate. But no one makes me angry. It is a response I choose based on my values, principles, beliefs, and core view of the world. The ideas in my head rule my actions and responses.

The proactive principle states that my body and soul may be a victim of abuse by others but my response to their abuse always remains in my control. Whatever people do to me they cannot rob me of my ability to choose a response. I am not responsible for their abuse, but I am responsible for my thoughts, words, actions, and attitudes following the abuse.

Now this assumes that they do not rob me of consciousness or rational thought due to forcing on me or tricking me into taking some type of drug or alcohol. Only once I am restored to my conscious and rational state do I regain my self control and determination. However, at that stage I am responsible for how I choose to respond to their abuse.

But, this is not how we feel most of the time. Our conversation is filled with statements like:

➤ You make me so happy!

➤ They made me mad!

➤ You caused me to be sad!

NEUROPHYSICAL MODEL OF MIND/BRAIN INTERACTION http://www-physics.lbl.gov/~stapp/PTB6.pdf

- ➤ You're driving me crazy!

- ➤ These circumstances are burning me out!

- ➤ If you had kept your mouth shut, I wouldn't have hit you!

In every case we act as though one person's actions forced upon us an inner state of thinking and drove us to actions that we could not control. But this is not really true.[6]

There are five general categories of events that normally tempt us to blame others for what we think, do, say and feel. These five categories are listed below, along with examples of events that tempt us to feel controlled by them rather than having a choice on how we will respond. These categories reflect some of the hardest and most painful moments in our lives.

---

[6] Only involuntary physical responses are outside our control. We have "knee jerk" reactions biologically to some stimulus.

- ➤ Moments of powerlessness

  - ○ Death of a loved one

  - ○ Serious or incurable illness of ourselves or a loved one

  - ○ Abuse which occurred to us as children

- ➤ Moments of homelessness

  - ○ Loss of a job

  - ○ Loss of property and possessions due to a natural disaster

  - ○ Financial ruin

- ➤ Moments of rootlessness

  - ○ Divorce

  - ○ All living relatives are dead or alienated

  - ○ Betrayal by friends or family

- ➤ Moments of hopelessness

  - ○ Death of a dream or vision

  - ○ Business failure

  - ○ Seeking to love another and being rejected

- ➤ Moments of meaninglessness

  - ○ Loss of ability or skill

  - ○ Loss of youth

  - ○ Loss of feeling productive[7]

---

[7] Kelly, *Christian Lore, Caring Community: A design for ministry*, (Chicago; Loyola University, 1983, pg xii.

These experiences will cause us pain. But, it is up to us to determine how we will respond to that pain. We can either have a sane, stable, and spiritual response or one that is dysfunctional and destructive. We cannot normally control the circumstances of our life but we can control our response to them. Positive thinking does not keep those we love from dying or our business from failing due to a national economic depression.

The main point is that when such things happen, most of us feel we are being controlled by the circumstances. The proactive principle teaches that while recognizing we cannot control many circumstances; we can control our response to the circumstances. Our responses are under our control.

Because of the overwhelming pain of some aspects in life, we are prone to excuse ourselves from acting in a sane, stable, and spiritual manner when these things occur. This becomes an excuse to also see far less traumatic events controlling our actions and words. Soon, we may blame shift more of what we say, feel and do to others. For some of us, we seldom take personal responsibility for anything. On the one hand, we feel less guilty and on the other we feel powerless all the time.

It is easier for most people to respond in dysfunctional and destructive ways than in sane, stable, and spiritual ways. It is often easier to blame others than to accept our own guilt.[8] But just because something is easier does not make it better. But wait a minute? Don't our genetics control us? The proactive principle believes that our behavioral genetic makeup may make it harder for us to avoid some destructive actions but does not force us to act in that way. Some people may be genetically inclined to become alcoholics but this does not excuse them from the responsibility to recognize this and abstain from drinking.

This is true unless a genetic defect robs us of our rationality. However, as long as we have our ability to think logically, then having a genetic inclination towards a behavior does not take from us the duty to avoid this behavior if it is destructive. Behavioral genetics, except those that steal from us our rationality, never have forced anyone to act in a certain way; they just make some ways of acting easier for us than others.

Well Ok, but is it not true we are controlled by our environment? The proactive principle would believe that our

---

[8] Some people accept guilt for things that others do. This is also against the proactive principle. Every person is responsible for their own wrong doing. We are never the cause for another person's dysfunctional and destructive actions.

home of origin and environment makes it easier for us to act in a particular way, but it does not predestine us to live out that life script we were given by our home environment. We can, as adults decide to re-write our "programs" and discard the "operating systems" that were given to us by our family and culture. If we change "the script" we change the "drama" of our life stories. We can rewrite the mental scripts given to us by those who raised us.

To buy into a proactive philosophy of life means we come to accept the reality that we are 100% responsible for what we do, say, and our attitudes. We refuse to shift blame to anyone else regardless of how abused we may be. It means we don't put our energy into what is "fair", but rather on how to find solutions. We don't look at what others are not doing for us, but rather what we could do ourselves. Our perspective is to not see ourselves as "victimized" but rather see ourselves as the responsible managers of our life and its resources.

What are the advantages of accepting a proactive approach to live? Without this principle, then we are helpless to take any action that would lead us to a more healthy and effective existence. While free of responsibility, we are also free of any meaningful power. We are adrift in the "river of life" with no more influence over our actions than a log floating down a river. The proactive principle is the foundational principle for everything else, as we seek to find greater sanity, stability, and spirituality.

ILLUSTRATION OF THE PRINCIPLE

There was a young man named Chris in a small private Christian school that has been set up in one of the poorest neighborhoods in America. The culture in which he lived was one of anger, violence, vice, and dysfunction. Chris was being raised by his mother.

Chris walked into fifth grade testing out at a third grade level. He was called "retarded" by the other children and acted as a person who had severe mental illness. He wore his clothing backwards and would just break out in laughter without any understandable reason. He called himself a retard. The "educational system" was just allowing him to be passed through the grades. They had given up on him. His mother wanting something better had come to the private Christian school and been awarded a scholarship so that he could attend. The school was there to serve the community and provide a safer, saner, more stable, and spiritual alternative to the education found at the public school in that area.

Chris' teacher did not accept the idea that he was retarded. There were inconstancy in his records and his actions. He began to pray for wisdom about how to help Chris.

When Chris was isolated from the other students the extreme behavior dropped off and conversations became more normal. The teacher began to tell Chris. "You have a good mind. You can't fool me, you're really very bright. I believe you could accomplish anything you wanted to do." The teacher became convinced that what Chris was suffering from was a learning disability.

Working with Chris's mother, seeking help from experts in learning disabilities, and observing Chris's behavior very carefully they began to develop methods that began to greatly help Chris learning. Chris also began to believe that he had choices to make about whether he did learn or did not learn. He stopped believing he was a "victim" of what he called his "bad brain" and decided to fully engage himself in the methods being used to help him.

The teacher was able to work with Chris for two years since in the small school he taught both the fifth and sixth grades together. By the end of the sixth grade Chris was now working on grade level, had an "A" in all his classes, and won an award for his outstanding work in math. He dressed differently and acted "normal".

Today, Chris is a missionary doctor providing vitally needed medical help to some of the poorest people in the third world. All of this because became possible because a teacher had a perspective that saw the potential within Chris, made a decision to seek to release that potential, and sought for methods to help Chris release that which was inside of him. The teacher was solution oriented rather than blaming, "the system" or the family. Rather than wasting energy on it all being "unfair", the teacher looked for ways to make things better. This was a proactive approach to the problem.

The key here however is not the teacher. The teacher had no power to move Chris from acting from a retarded person to being a medical doctor. That power was within Chris by the grace of God. If Chris decided to continue to see himself as a victim of a "bad brain" then he might well be living underneath a bridge today. It was because Chris accepted a proactive outlook on his life and decided that he could adapt to the brain he had been given with its learning disabilities and overcome them, that his world changed. This is allowing Chris to live a productive and whole life. By the way, the teacher who helped Chris also has a learning disability.

WHAT IS THIS PROACTIVE ATTITUDE?

To incorporate a proactive mind frame into the fiber of our being we must look at it in the light of sanity, stability, and spirituality.

- ❖ Our seeing must be sane,
- ❖ our vision must be stable,
- ❖ and our insight must be spiritual

For us to successfully use a proactive point of view into the midst of our real life challenges and problems we must see reality for what it is, practice a stable vision of reality, and have insight about the purpose and plan of life. Only when each of these elements is rightly aligned do we get the results we need from accepting a proactive philosophy of life.

SANE SEEING

Sanity is to see reality as it really is and desire to adapt to reality appropriately. It means that we very objectively determine what is under our control and what is not under our control. Rather than seeing ourselves powerless victims we need to see that our power is always the same. It is the power to control ourselves from the inside out.

Now, because we have lived in an insane environment which encourages reactive thinking this very sane and real approach it hard for us to accept. We will have to diligently reinforce this belief and consciously decide to reinterpret events so that we will train our minds to see things from a proactive point of view. We must correct every random "reactive" statement with a reality check in which we tell ourselves the truth that we our actions, thoughts, words, and emotions are not given to us but chosen by us.[9] Here are some examples of how we might do this.

I Say	I Correct Myself
She/He made me so mad!	I choose to become mad in response to what they said
I had to lie because I knew how they would react	I choose to lie because I decided to not deal with their reaction to the truth

---

[9] It is admitted that sometimes the chemistry in our body is the source of our emotional states. Some of these are normal and others abnormal. In some cases due to a dysfunction of our brain or chemistry we may experience states of being which are totally ruled by involuntary chemical process. However, once we begin to admit this reality we have a great ability to proactively decide to govern the effects of these chemical processes and still strive to become whole in heart and mind. See the movie and read the book "A Beautiful Mind."

She/He makes me so happy!	She/He is acting in a positive manner and I am choosing to respond to them in a positive manner
I can't live without you!	I am making a choice to not live without you
I can't work with such an incompetent boss	I am choosing to sabotage my work to express my frustration with my boss
You frustrate me!	I am choosing to lose patience with you in the hope of changing you
She/He never lets me do what I want!	I choose to do what the other person wants to avoid conflict.

To see ourselves not in control of anyone but ourselves is a vital part of finding harmony in our inner life. Not only do others not control our inner reality, we do not control their inner reality either. Each person is responsible for the state of their inner reality and the actions they choose to take in order to cope with the issues they face. Our choices are our "coping" methods. They are the means by which we hope to conquer the problems of our life.

Once we recognize these methods are being chosen by us and not forced upon us, it becomes easier to evaluate if the methods we are choosing are actually the best methods for the circumstances. As we go further in the process, this becomes vital to the setting of our priorities. Yet, we can only begin to choose better methods once we are deeply convinced we are proactively responsible for our entire inner reality and all our actions. Only when thinking from a proactive perspective is habitual will this principle regularly help us succeed at life.

We accomplish this by carefully watching over our thoughts and words along with rejecting the old "reactive" programming. We can also use positive self-talk as a way to reinforce this new way of seeing life. This self talk may look something like this.

Self Talk To Gain A Proactive Life

- ❖ I have control over my thoughts

- ❖ I can change my thoughts where I do not believe

  they work for my best interests

- ❖ I can reject unhealthy or abusive thoughts

- ❖ I can reject thoughts which are unrealistic and false

- ❖ I can control my words

- ❖ I can think before I speak

- ❖ I can control my actions

- ❖ I can think before I act

- ❖ I can choose my attitude

- ❖ I can be focused on finding solutions

- ❖ I can look how to find positive aspects in the middle

  of hard circumstances

- ❖ I am not responsible for what other people think,

  do, or say

By saying this to ourselves six times each day for ninety days we will begin to reprogram our perspective on life to one that allows us to consciously use our power of self control. This exercise allows us to evaluate our actions, words, and attitudes in a sane, proactive manner. Another example of this type of self talk is given in the exercises at the end of this chapter. Write up your own self talk so that the words will be those that most work for you.

STABLE VISION

As we begin to accept this new way of thinking we must develop a lifestyle that reflects this outlook on life. To reprogram the reactive lifestyle we must reinforce and maintain diligence and effort to see life differently for at least 90 days. Habits govern our lives. They are vehicles our minds use to take shortcuts. Most of the actions we take are little more than entrenched habits. We operate on automatic pilot most of the time. This is one of the reasons we do not feel very "proactive" in our daily existence, since we feel more driven by the routines of life than voluntarily making significant choices.

At some point in our life we had to choose those activities and thought patterns that are now habitual. We choose to make this the normal program for our daily lifestyle. We forgot that we this pattern is one we have adopted to be our program. But that does not make it any less a preference for how we interpret life.

We can now use this habitual habit of the brain to our advantage. We can choose to make a proactive approach to life our normal pattern of living and thinking. The key here is consistency and repetition. We must actively seek to "reject" every reactive thought with a gentle rebuke and reward every proactive impulse with great praise. The exercises we use to help us have sane seeing must be reinforced over at least a 90 day period in order for the habitual patterns of our thinking to change.

Another exercise we can do is accomplished by simply writing out our normal weekly schedule. Put down on a piece of paper all the events of your week. You can even do this at the end of the week after everything has happened, or you can do it at the beginning before anything has occurred. On the list of events that make up your week, simply write before each event the words "I choose".

For example:
- ➤ I choose to wake up at 6 am on Monday morning.
- ➤ I choose to not eat breakfast.
- ➤ I choose to go to work today.
- ➤ I choose to brush my teeth today.
- ➤ I choose to exercise today.
- ➤ I choose to gossip about my boss today.
- ➤ I choose to meet with a client at noon.
- ➤ I choose to come home to my family today.

Doing this exercise weekly or even daily could be a very powerful reinforcement of the proactive truth. Ultimately, we are choosing our lifestyles and the events in our lives. Our daily patterns are there because we have chosen them to be there at this present moment.

As you go through this exercise, you may feel there should be different events in your life than really exist. That is very normal. Later we will look at methods to help you abandon unwanted patterns. Right now, you may want to note which of your patterns you feel comfortable with and which ones feel less comfortable. Did your lack of comfort become greater because you said "I choose"? Many times this is the case. We have accepted some of our actions and activities because we felt powerless. Once we recognize we are not powerless, it is harder to accept some of the things we do on a regular basis. But, that is a good insight and one that will help empower desired change later on.

To stabilize our sane vision of being proactive, responsible adults will require regular exercises used to strengthen our perception of not being driven to have to take actions through circumstances beyond our control. Just as regular resistant exercise is the process by which our physical muscles grow, so regular mental and emotional exercises are the only way we can become inwardly healthier and stronger. Make it your intention to stabilize your proactive vision into a regular habit in your life.

SPIRITUAL INSIGHT

The Serenity Prayer

God grant me the serenity
To accept the things I cannot change;
Courage to change the things I can;
And wisdom to know the difference.

Living one day at a time;
Enjoying one moment at a time;
Accepting hardships as the pathway to peace;
Taking, as Jesus did, this sinful world
As it is, not as I would have it;

Trusting that He will make all things right
If I surrender to His will;
That I may be reasonably happy in this life
And supremely happy with Him
Forever in the next.
Amen.

This prayer has become best known because of its wide use in Alcoholics Anonymous and Narcotics Anonymous groups around the world. It is prayer to have God help me to accept a very proactive approach to life. I find there are things outside my control. Things I cannot change. These are the actions of others and the circumstances of my existence. I cannot change the past. These I do not control. I waste my energy by attempting to control them or change them.

But, the prayer is also very clear that I must be able to see the things I do control. There are some things I can change. I can gain self control. I do control what I think, do, say, and my attitudes. This is where I can make positive change. This is where I should put my focus, prayers, and energy. I can find my peace and contentment by not rejecting this reality, but fully accepting it. Part of my process is to ask for God's help in coming to this recognition.[10]   One tool to use in gaining this perspective is to purposely and emotionally pray this prayer for ninety days once in the morning and another time right before you go to bed. This will begin to sell your "soul" or subconscious into this reality and help you focus your prayers on this vital issue looking to God to help you change inside.

Part of this recognition is we need to trust God to manage the universe and accept that God has trusted us with the job to manage ourselves.[11]   We have a limited amount of energy and time. If we spend time and energy attempting to control others and circumstances outside of our control, we will not have the time and energy needed to effectively maintain and live a life of self control. We can see this in the following diagram:

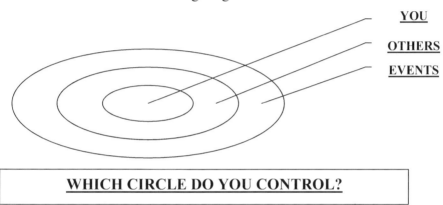

| WHICH CIRCLE DO YOU CONTROL? |

The more time and energy I spend on attempting to control others and having anxiety about circumstances, the less I have to give to the development of my sanity, stability, and spirituality. The less I put into the development of my thoughts and emotions, the less self control I exercise. This makes my sphere of influence smaller and smaller.

Imagine that all the energy and strength we have could be described as "100 Life Units". If we spend 80 of the "Life Units"

---

[10] For those who struggle with God's existence and prayer, I would recommend reading *Yes or No?: Straight Answers to Tough Questions About Christianity* and *Prayer: The Great Conversation: Straight Answers to Tough Questions About Prayer* by Dr. Peter Kreeft, teacher of philosophy at Boston College. If God is part of reality, then the only sane way to adapt to him is to pray to him. See also Appendix on "Matters of Faith."

[11] Self control is really only possible because of the grace of God and the filling of the Holy Spirit. This is done through the means of our living a disciplined and wise life. We need God's strength to succeed.

attempting to control others and events, then this leads us only 20 "Life Units" of strength and energy to control ourselves. We will find when we do invest our "Life Units" in this way that we do poorly in managing our own actions, words, and attitudes. However, if our focus is to put 80 of our "Life Units" of energy and strength into gaining self control we will manage our lives much better and feel we are experiencing a very sane, stable, and spiritual life. We must be aware of where we are investing our "Life Units" of energy and recognize we are very limited in resources. We dare not waste our strength on that which we cannot control. Part of our prayer is that we will have the spiritual insight to release to God those things outside of our control, so that we may have the strength to be good managers of the life He has given to us.

The New Testament aids us in dealing with the anxiety over events outside our control in what has historically been called "the prayer of release." We find this described in a letter to the church in the city of Philippi by a wise spiritual director the Apostle Paul.

> "Do not be anxious about anything, but in everything by prayer and supplication with thanksgiving let your requests be made known to God. And the peace of God, which surpasses all understanding, will guard your hearts and your minds in Christ Jesus. Finally, brothers, whatever is true, whatever is honorable, whatever is just, whatever is pure, whatever is lovely, whatever is commendable, if there is any excellence, if there is anything worthy of praise, think about these things. What you have learned and received and heard and seen in me - practice these things, and the God of peace will be with you." Philippians 4:6-9 ESV

Here we find that inner peace is found by releasing into God's care all the circumstances outside of my control and all the destructive actions of people in my life. By recognizing I have no control over these events but trusting that in some way God will use all of these dysfunctional and hurtful events towards some ultimate good, allows me to have inner psychological peace.

In addition, I am also asked not to think in black and white categories. Not all the actions of others are bad and dysfunctional. Not all the circumstances of my life are hurtful. Sane thinking is not making reality better than it is, but also not making it worse.

By purposely focusing on what is going right instead of what is going wrong, I again gain psychological clarity and calmness. In both areas of releasing anxiety and avoiding unrealistic depression, the spiritual aspect of reality aids us in developing and deepening our proactive perspective on life.

SUMMARY

Proactive processing of life circumstances requires us to perceive and envision life in a very sane and stable manner. This perspective is greatly aided as we look at the larger spiritual perspective helps us see our significant, but limited responsibility. By consistent focus and practice we can develop a proactive foundation upon which the development of a succeeding approach to life can be based. Once we have firmly established this vision of personal responsibility, we are ready to process the past wounds of our life, so they do not keep us from succeeding at life.

Chapter One Exercises

1. One of the ways our entire mind adopts a new outlook is by spaced repletion. This is a Hebrew form of meditation (*hagah*) which means to "mutter to one's self". By repeating truth to ourselves, our conscious mind speaks to our inner reality and begins to reprogram our thinking with a new outlook on life. Here are suggested self talk "meditations" to see in a sane way or proactive nature.

> - I am responsible for what I think.
> - I am responsible for what I do.
> - I am responsible for what I say.
> - I am responsible for how I respond.
> - I have more than one option on how I can respond to circumstances.
> - I can choose my response.
> - I am never forced to make an abusive or harmful response by someone else.
> - I am never forced to make an abusive or harmful response by something else.
> - I am free to choose my responses to life's joys and sorrows.
> - My freedom depends on my ability to choose a response
> - I want to be free.
> - Therefore, I want to be responsible for my own actions and words.

The ideal way to make this work is to say this out loud three times a day while looking in a mirror. Attempt to put genuine emotion into the reading. What we say with passion sticks longer in our brain than when we lack passion. You could also have this on an index card and read it whenever you catch yourself in reactive thinking. Use of these "meditations" for ninety days could help you radically change your viewpoint and open up a whole new door to your understanding in daily life. You should write up your own version of this self talk so that it will be personalized and reflect your personal ideas and convictions.

2. There is a very ancient prayer tradition related to the prayer of release. Some refer to it as "palms down & palms up". This is how you would go through this ritual;

- Find a place of solitude and quiet.
- Sit in a comfortable manner.
- Take a deep breath and release your stress as you breathe out.
- Put your hands in front of you and make fists with your palms towards the ground.
- In your mind, imagine all the worry, concern, frustration, and anger you have because of what others are doing. Now imagine this worry, concern, frustration, and anger moving down your arms and into your clenched fists.
- In your mind, imagine all the worry, concern, frustration, and anger you have because of difficult circumstances. Now imagine this worry, concern, frustration, and anger moving down your arms and into your clenched fists.
- Feel your fists getting heavier as they hold onto your burdens.
- Take time to do this so you are very focused on seeing in your mind this actually happening.
- Take a deep breath.
- Now, lift your hands towards the sky and turn your palm up and open your hands. In your mind, see your anxieties and worries over people and circumstances flowing out of your hands into the hands of God.
- As you do this, keep repeating "Into Your hands, I release my worries and fears".
- Keep your hands lifted until you feel the weight of your worries lifted.
- Take a deep breath.
- Thank God for taking your burdens from you.
- Ask God for the strength to focus your strength on your duties and not on your worries.

Doing this once a day for 90 days can help you see there is another method for handling your anxiety about other people and circumstances. This allows you to now put your limited energy on obtaining self control and your own inner peace.

Seeing God as one who cares for us allows us to live with fewer cares. Experiment with this process.

Memorize this verse as a focus point in doing this exercise:

"Casting all your anxiety upon Him, because He cares for you." 1 Peter 5:7 NAS

Chapter One Journal - What thoughts, feelings, impressions, questions, or musings came through this chapter?

_____

_____

_____

_____

_____

_____

_____

_____

_____

_____

_____

_____

_____

_____

_____

_____

Chapter Two: Past Wounds

Past wounds – Experiences we remember where we suffered a loss. Wounds were moments of powerlessness, homelessness, rootlessness, hopelessness, and meaninglessness. From this pain, we have created proverbs, life principles, and significant parts of the interpretive grid through which we make current decisions. Our past wounds are impacting our present lives. The stories we have created around these events have become part of the "mental script" by which we live. Our interpretation of these events generates thoughts and emotions that become the basis for our daily actions.

MAIN PURPOSE OF CHAPTER TWO:

To provide a practical approach to defining and dealing with the pain of the past so it will not hinder us from succeeding at life.

OPENING EXERCISE:

Think in your mind about the person who has had the most negative impact on your life, the person who comes to your thoughts when you think of pain, abuse, hurt, sorrow, betrayal, or trauma. Envision in your mind this person and the impact he or she had on your life. Now imagine this person had a radically different personality. Whatever they did to hurt you, they did not do. Whatever words they spoke that injured you, they did not speak. In fact, the deeds and words that come from them in your mind are the ideal words and deeds they should have done. How does this impact you? How would your life be different today? How does this exercise make you feel?

BASIC THOUGHTS:

It would be nice to think we can just forget the past and move on. This is the temptation to "stuff it". We strive to not think about the past or remember those things that hurt us. We rationalize this with statements such as, "I survived, and so what is the big deal?"

As long as the past influences our decisions in the present, it is not past. Much of our personal "wisdom" comes because of the interpretation or stories we tell about past events. Some of the "wisdom" might be wise; but some of this "wisdom" might be insanity.

For example, a friend or lover betrays us, so we vow to ourselves we will never be emotionally intimate again. We repeat to ourselves self-made proverbs such as, "You can't trust anyone." These were formed out of the times of trauma. Many times, the pain caused by a bad event changed us in a far greater way than the original trauma; we then use this pain as the interpretive grid of reality. As proactive people we need to evaluate our experiences and the life principles they spawned and assess whether we are happy with what we concluded in the midst of our pain. This does not happen with just "stuffing it."

Remembering and dealing with past memories and emotional wounds can cause us to panic, because we fear they can destroy us. The reason we seldom logically and sanely deal with past hurts is because inwardly it seems they have the power to psychologically destroy us. The reason we run from them is that the memories which hold our pain scare us like a million magnified nightmares. We think the only way to survive is never to fully face them.

Yet, the reality is we have already survived the real historical trauma. All that is left is a "ghost of a memory", which is still haunting our minds and bringing us pain today. The best way to see these ghosts exorcised is not by running from them, but to confront them in a loving, but firm way until we gain inward peace and personal wholeness between our past and present realities. This provides a secure starting point in the present to succeed at life.

ILLUSTRATION OF THE PRINCIPLE

There was a young man who was raised in an alcoholic home. The home was filled with physical, emotional, and verbal abuse. His family believed his birth was the cause of all the conflict in the home. He was told as a young child that before he was born, they had a happy home. He was a sickly and weak child. His father regularly communicated his disappointment at having such a worthless son. When the divorce occurred, his mother told him the reason for the divorce was concern over his deep depression. His weakness was seen as the justification for the ending of the marriage. In response to this, the young man chose to hate himself and accepted the blame placed upon him. There were many times when he wanted to commit suicide in order to "atone" for his birth and end his unbearable pain. Only the fear of being condemned to hell if he committed suicide kept the young man alive.

The young man became a hard worker in the hope of feeling worthy of existence. He excelled in school and was an activist for causes that helped the hurting, weak, and poor. He also found he became co-dependent and needy in relationships. He wanted his friends and lovers to constantly assure him he was significant and he lived for their approval. He became an approval addict. Many relationships were ruined by the dysfunctional pressure he placed on them. His inward world was filled with self hatred and depression, even though he had some signs of outward success.

Reflecting on his life, he decided he had to deal with the wounds of his past to succeed at life. A spiritual mentor began helping him and he started journaling his feelings about the past. The unspoken feelings were written. He put new dimensions on the memories he had of the past and visited his childhood from the perspective of a healthy adult observer. Slowly, he began to see his childhood from a realistic and sane perspective.

Through a process of prayer, small group dynamics, meditation, and journaling he experienced a substantial healing of his inner reality. He now lives a well balanced life and is not driven to prove his worth. He has come to appreciate and like the person God made him to be. The painful past that nearly drove him to suicide and hindered him from finding balance, has now been proactively processed. He feels he is now in a daily process of succeeding at life.

SANE EVALUATION

A sane evaluation of our past wounds means we must evaluate what type of wound we suffered and how severe this emotional pain was in our lives. Some of us experienced sexual abuse, physical abuse, verbal abuse, religious abuse and/or emotional abuse. Our experience was filled with feelings of powerlessness, homelessness, rootlessness, hopelessness, and meaninglessness. Our family who was to provide security and unconditional acceptance became the source of condemnation, rejection, and abandonment. Because we suffered some of this pain while we were young, dependent, and developing we were less able to make wise choices about how to respond to the pain. Some of us have also suffered trauma not associated with our families of origin.

But this trauma still has caused us deep pain. We began to interpret the world in dysfunctional and destructive ways. Most of the time, this inner pain from wounds has become jumbled up in our minds, and is creating hurt we try to ignore so we can survive in the present. Ignoring the pain has not made the emotional tenderness or negative influences from the past leave. We find ourselves fragmented and distorted because of this inner ache of our souls.

Our fear of facing the pain of the past stems from falsely believing it has the power to destroy our present. We bury this pain because we fear it will be more than we could handle. We may have used alcohol, drugs, impersonal or excessive sexuality, pornography, co-dependent relationships, excessive work, excessive hobbies, or even crusading for good causes in an attempt to run from our past emotional wounds. Many of these extreme activities of great "sinners" and "saints" have been a way to overload the present so we don't have to deal with the inner wounds of the past. This leads to "excessive" and "imbalanced" living. When we recognize we have already survived the past and all that is left of that terrible time is a shadow of a memory, we can face and accept our past hurt without fear of melting down in the present.

The pain of our past can be characterized under two broad

headings:

> Pain we had no control over because it was caused by someone else or circumstances;

and

> Pain we caused ourselves by foolish and dysfunctional actions.

To begin this process, we need to list all the significant moments of pain we remember and evaluate them objectively.

Some will say they do not remember much of their childhood. Others have a feeling that they have suppressed memories of bad events. There is much debate about suppressed memories[12]. However, people in counseling have had experiences where traumatic events are "remembered" that had been "forgotten" since before the time of Sigmund Freud.

We should not try to find forgotten memories. But if they come to us, they need to be considered as potentially real events. It is always best to find outside objective confirmation since it is possible for our minds to fool us. However, we need to face the fact that anything that is remembered is real to the person who remembers it. Every painful memory will have to be processed as though it is real, unless it can be shown to be false.

The following chart may help. List the wounds and put them in the column they fit best. Then on a scale from one to ten with ten being the greatest impact, determine how significant each past wound is to your current lifestyle and is hindering you from moving toward your deepest desires.

---

[12] http://depression.about.com/b/2007/07/17/area-of-brain-responsible-for-suppressed-memories-located.htm

Age of wound	Caused by someone or something else	Caused by me	Level of current impact this event has on my life

You can duplicate this chart if you need more space. The key is to summarize and evaluate the past pain and the impact it is having on your current life.

Now fill out the chart believing in the proactive principle. Do not blame yourself for the actions, words, or attitudes of others. Remember, you are only responsible for what you have done and said.

Now it is time to also face the pain caused by our own actions. This is done by making a radical moral inventory of our lives. You can do a radical moral inventory by filling out the following chart in your journal.

List times when I failed what I believe God desired to be done in my life?	
List times when I failed to act in a loving way towards my family?	
List times when I failed to act in a loving way towards my friends?	
List times when I abused other people physically, emotionally, or verbally	
List times when I lied	
List times when I stole	
List times when I used sex selfishly and not as an act of love	
List times when I gossiped about others	
List times when I acted foolishly and it had bad consequences	
List any other events that I feel brought hurt to others and/or myself	

Now the key here again is the proactive principle. Fully own what you have done. Do not blame anyone else. Accept that you are 100% responsible for your deeds and actions. At this point it would be wise to remember a promise found in the Bible:

> "But if we walk in the light, as he is in the light, we
> have fellowship with one another, and the blood of
> Jesus his Son cleanses us from all sin. If we say we

have no sin, we deceive ourselves, and the truth is
not in us. If we confess our sins, he is faithful and
just to forgive us our sins and to cleanse us from all
unrighteousness. If we say we have not sinned, we
make him a liar, and his word is not in us." (1 John
1:6-9)

I have heard it said that Martin Luther once remarked that we can
confess boldly because God boldly forgives us in Christ Jesus. By
having a real faith in God's forgiveness of our sins we can also
claim responsibility for our sins without blame shifting to others in
any way. To be sane we must not deny our responsibility for the
painful actions we have taken.

STABLE PROCESS

As you list the past wounds, you need to ask yourself a
question. Is the pain of my past more than I can process without
assistance? We must determine if the impact of our past is
significant enough for us to seek professional help. There is no
shame in seeking such help. Many times a counselor can shorten
the process and make it more effective. The work you have
already done in listing and evaluating your past wounds will
greatly help a professional counselor work with you to help
overcome the impact of the painful past on your current life.

With or without professional help, there are some tools
which provide a stable processing of the wounds of our past so
they no longer have significant impact on our present. One
proactive tool to deal with the past is through directed journaling.
Some of the journaling exercises that can help are the following:

> Imagine your life is a novel. Separate your life into
> chapters. The divisions are whatever seem meaningful to
> you. Under each section, set aside the most significant
> events both positive and negative. Give each "chapter" of
> your book a title. After you have worked through your life
> up to the present, give your entire life a title. Also,
> summarize under each section any "life rules" , "personal
> proverbs", "vows", or "life lessons" that came about
> because of a particular incident. As you look at these "life
> principles", ask yourself if you are satisfied this represents

the values and operating systems of your life? Would you be happy if your children or those most precious to you lived their lives by these precepts? Why or why not?

➤ Also, take each of the significant events and write your thoughts, feelings, questions, and musings about it. Write about the event until you have nothing left in you to write about it.

➤ Write letters in your journal to those who hurt you. You can express your anger, hurt, disappointment, and confusion.

➤ Write a prayer letter to God and express your feelings about circumstances that brought you great pain. You can express confusion, admit anger, and ask for help in understanding why God allowed this event to occur.

Another way of proactively dealing with the past is through the use of imagination. In this process, a person imagines he is going back in time as a mature adult to the time when he was hurt as a child. As an adult, he interprets what is happening and imagines explaining to the child these events from the perspective of a caring and sympathetic adult. In this way we can parent ourselves. This "time travel" approach can help us gain fresh perspective and come to terms with many underlying issues. This particular process is most helpful when done with a trained counselor.

Finally, we can proactively process the past by confrontation of those who abused us and revisiting the actual physical place where we suffered our pain. If we believe that such a confrontation can be done safely we may find it helps us to directly and responsibly share our feelings with those who hurt us. We must do this with no expectation of how the other person will react.

The success of this process does not depend on the person who hurt us. The fact we can confront them and tell them how we feel is freeing and enables us to move forward. This is not always wise or practical, but in some cases it is very helpful. Again, if you have any doubts this would be a good idea, get feedback from a professional counselor about what would be the best course of action.

It is important to be systematic when working on past wounds and to only focus on one at a time. We can only process so much so fast. We must be patient with the process. At times events may be clustered because they highlight one person, so we need to deal with them all at once.

In dealing with pain we have caused ourselves the real focus we should have is on learning from our past actions. What can I do from responding to life in a negative and destructive way today? What patterns are there in my "self destructive" actions which I need to be careful about not repeating? How could I change my response to similar circumstances today? The goal is in learning to not repeat mistakes.

The key here is in being realistic and kind to yourself. Don't try to process more than you are able. Slow and steady succeeds in winning the race when it comes to making peace with our painful past. Again, it is important to remember we survived the "real" event and now we are attempting to cope with the emotions the memory of this event stirs up in us. Overcoming the memory is easier than surviving the event. By systematically providing time to process our painful past, we can make peace with it, receive healing and be well positioned to succeed in life now.

SPIRITUAL HEALING

When dealing with the past, we face three key issues:

> ➤ First, it is hard to be at peace with people who have hurt us;
> ➤ Secondly, it is hard to not be mad at God for allowing bad things to happen;
> ➤ Thirdly, it is hard to feel forgiven when we know our own mistakes and foolishness caused ourselves and others pain.

These three issues are some of the main reasons we keep these events buried.

Letting go of the pain others have caused is difficult if we seek a just resolution. Sometimes, the person who hurt us will offer a sincere apology. However, this is rare. Most people justify their actions or deny they ever happened. Rarely, does the person who hurt us suffer any just consequences for their actions.

Because of this, we have a tendency to keep rehearsing the injustice over and over again. This leads to a state of bitterness and anger. If the wounded person turns this anger inward, the anger becomes depression. If it is turned outward, the danger becomes expressing anger inappropriately towards others. Focusing on judgment leads to elevated stress, anxiety, frustration, and rage. Therefore, we must let go of "fairness" and instead deal with how to help ourselves from suffering in the present moment due to the unjust things we have suffered.

It is important for us to become solution-oriented and decide to let go of the bitterness and anger. We should find a "sympathetic ear". This can be found many times in a pastor or spiritual director. It is important to have someone sympathetically listen to our pain.

After this we then should use the prayer of release to let go of this painful experience[13]. We should release the offender to God and not allow vengeful thoughts. To hold on to anger and vengeance is like holding a burning coal in your lap…. it is going to cause you a lot of pain and damage! Only when we admit these feelings are causing personal harm, will we find the power to let them go.

Most of us also blame God for circumstances that brought us harm. Whether it's the death of a lost one or being fired from a job, we may interpret this as God failing us by allowing painful events into our lives. Forgiving God is hard, because most of us deny we are angry at him. As stated when we discussed journaling, we can express our feelings to God since He is already aware of our struggles.

It may also help to read some books on this subject such as C.S. Lewis' *The Problem of Pain* [14] or Peter Kreeft's, *Making Sense Out of Suffering*,[15] which address how we can believe in a God who is all powerful and good, but experience pain and evil in the world. Sometimes, our inner reality can be comforted and reconciled by getting better answers than the ones we currently hold. This aspect of bringing wholeness to our inner world has rarely been discussed, but is vital. Some atheists are really

---

[13] See chapter two

[14] CS Lewis, *The Problem of Pain* (New York: Macmillan, 1944, Harper Collins, edition 2001)

[15] Peter Kreeft, *Making Sense Out of Suffering* (Ann Arbor Michigan: Servant Books, 1986)

disappointed and hurt people who have turned from God in anger.[16]

It is also important we feel forgiven. Sometimes, this means we recognize our guilt was really a false sense of guilt. We were assuming responsibility for someone else's wrong. At other times, we must face foolish, abusive, and hurtful things we did and accept without excuse our responsibility. Forgiving ourselves seems like a "cop out" of responsibility, but it is part of the healing process and a critical component to properly applied Christian faith, helping us succeed at life. If we demand perfection from ourselves then we will destroy ourselves with self hatred and condemnation.

One of the most helpful aspects of Christian faith is it offers us a clear road on how to forgive ourselves and others. The Christian worldview tells us confession is "good for the soul" and provides forgiveness by God which allows us to move on. As I noted earlier we do have a promise from God that can help us.

> *"If we say we have no sin, we deceive ourselves, and the truth is not in us. [9] If we confess our sins, He is faithful and just to forgive us our sins and to cleanse us from all unrighteousness. [10] If we say we have not sinned, we make Him a liar, and His word is not in us."* 1 John 1:8 ESV

Confession is the application of the proactive principle before God. We admit we did wrong and were one hundred percent responsible for the wrong without excuses. Confession also includes a desire to not repeat the mistake and also the desire to make restitution to the person we harmed if practical and advisable. But, there is also a cleansing of the past and the ability to move on to the future. According to the Christian worldview, this was what Jesus Christ accomplished by his death for those who believe. His death paid the price for our moral failure and allows a just forgiveness of our sins.

While those outside the Christian worldview find the death of Jesus Christ as a payment for sins mysterious and even foolish, it nevertheless laid the foundation for a just forgiveness of sins and the reunion and communion with God for all who have done

---

[16] Exline, J.J., & Martin, A. (2005). Anger toward God: A new frontier in forgiveness research. In E.L. Worthington, Jr. (ed.), Handbook of Forgiveness (pp73-88). New York: Routledge.

wrong. It also provides a justification to forgive ourselves. If such a sacrifice is enough for a perfectly righteous God to grant pardon, how can we not believe it is sufficient for us to forgive ourselves? These emotional processes take time and faith, but here is one example where the Christian worldview provides a firm foundation of restoration for succeeding at life.

It will be difficult to make peace with your past without dealing with the issue of forgiveness. Only by releasing others and ourselves from the demands of vengeance can we move on to a peaceful present. Where the person has not repented we can still choose to "love our enemies" and do good to those who have abused us without opening ourselves up to more abuse. This may not help our enemies but it will help us. The human heart must surrender its claims to justice and instead live in an atmosphere filled with mercy and grace to stay healthy.

SUMMARY

To find inward wholeness from the pain of the past, we must be willing to face the events of the past and carefully evaluate them. Once we abandon denial about the impact of our past on the present, we are ready to consistently and stably use the processes which help us emotionally reconcile our past. This may best be done with a counselor. As we actively become involved in this process, we will need to release others from the harm they may have done to us and to also forgive ourselves. This may take time, but our innermost self will find resolution with the losses of the past. We will be better prepared as we move on towards the future, anticipating we will succeed at life.

Notes

_____

_____

_____

Summary of how to overcome our painful past

1. Write up a summary of your life and think of it as a book. Think of each part of your life as a chapter. You can divide it anyway you think is best. Give each era of your life a title. Name the three main painful events of each era. Also make note of any special moments of happiness and joy. You can also give your whole life a title. This will give you a forest view of your life which may open up some new insights in how the parts of your life relate.

2. In your imagination visit the most painful events of your past as a sane, stable, and spiritual adult. Tell your younger self the truth about each event and comfort the memory of yourself the same way you would a child you loved.

3. Make a list of painful events where you were hurt and evaluate their impact on your life on a scale form 1-10.

4. Do a radical moral inventory of your life and own every action that caused someone else or yourself harm.

5. Seek to develop forgiveness as the key way to deal with past events. Accept God's forgiveness for your sins, come to peace with what God has allowed to happen in your life, and refuse to become bitter towards others.

6. Ask God to help you to make peace with the pain of your past.

7. Seek professional counseling to help you in this process.

Chapter Two Exercises

1. Are there people you need to communicate to about hurtful events? Perhaps you owe someone an "I'm sorry" or "I'm thankful for your helping me." Is there someone you need to confront over the hurt they caused you? Perhaps a carefully written letter edited by wise friends to the person who hurt you could be one way to release the pain.

2. The past is not just about pain. There have been good moments in our life as well as those that traumatized us. To avoid negative thinking, make a list of every goal you have accomplished, skill you have acquired, friend you have made, joy you have experienced, insight you have gained, burden you have shed, and victory you have won. Keep this list with you and read it whenever you feel down or overwhelmed.

3. Make a list of regrets you have about your life. Next to the regret write down either something you can do to make amends to the person or simply the words "nothing to be done." Read the regrets out loud and then read 1 John 1:9 out loud. Ask God to help you experience a sense of forgiveness through Jesus Christ.

4. Make a list of people that made positive contributions to your life. These could be parents, relatives, teachers, friends, and co-workers. Write a thank you note to each person and try to actually mail it. You will see there have been many allies to you along your journey.

Journal for chapter two

What thoughts, feelings, impressions, questions, or musings came through this chapter?

_____

_____

_____

_____

_____

_____

_____

_____

_____

_____

_____

_____

_____

_____

_____

_____

_____

_____

_____

_____

_____

_____

_____

_____

_____

_____

_____

_____

_____

_____

_____

_____

_____

_____

_____

The past is gone, the future is not yet, the only moment that actually exists is that cutting edge of reality we call 'the present.

Chapter Three: Present Reality

MAIN PURPOSE:

To help us define and evaluate our present personal reality so we may have a clear starting point towards succeeding at life.

OPENING EXERCISE:

Let yourself be focused only on this present time in your life. Close the door of the past and do not think about the future. Be only in the present. Imagine you are in an airplane and looking down on your present life. What do you see? How do you feel about what you see?

WELCOME TO TODAY!

The danger with looking at the past is we have a tendency to live in the past. Some people idolize the past and want to only talk about the "good old days" while others demonize the past as they talk about the darkness of their pain. While making peace with our past is part of having a successful attitude towards life, we must always focus in the present to actually succeed at life.

The most precious moment is now. The only space in time we really live is in this precious, present moment. We must recognize this present moment is all we have. We are not guaranteed the next. To savor and love our moment-by-moment existence is critical to succeeding at life. People often either dream about the future or dwell in past nostalgia or despair. Few people live in the NOW! If you want to succeed at life, you must live in the present moment with anticipation, joy, and purpose.

ILLUSTRATION

There was a man who lived in despair. His father had never believed he would succeed. Other members of the family had gained positions of wealth and power. His life course was to be a simple, blue collar worker. He did not attempt to have more financially than the other members of his family. His father always pointed out at family functions how his son was the "failure" of the family. He agreed with his father. He felt like a failure.

Talking to a spiritual director one day about these feelings of "failure" the director asked him some questions.

Question: Did you ever purpose to become wealthy and powerful?

Answer: No, I never really wanted to be rich. My family and I get by and that really was all I was ever after. This is most likely one of my problems. I just lack ambition.

Question: What goal did you want to attain?

Answer: I wanted to be a musician. My father thought this was crazy and did everything to discourage me. I knew there was no money in it, so I never became one.

Question: So you don't play music today?

Answer: No, I do play in worship teams around the city. I am very involved in a fellowship of Christian musicians who are very creative. But, I don't get paid for that.

Question: Is something worthless because you don't get paid?

Answer: I never thought about that. I guess not.

Question: Then your life time goal of what you wanted was to be a musician?

Answer: Yes, that was one of them.

Question: And if I hear you right, you have reached this goal and are enjoying it.

Answer: Well, now that you put it like that. Yes, I have actually attained what I had hoped to become.

Question: And your father still disapproves, but that is not all so surprising?

The man's eyes suddenly sparkled. He had achieved his dream of being a musician. As the director and the man began to take inventory of what he really did have in the present moment, they found he was a very rich and powerful man. The man was rich in friends and powerful in integrity. The real state of his life had been hidden by a negative evaluation given by his father. From that day, the depression left the man and he had joy and appreciation for his present life.

Sometimes we don't really know what we have until we take stock. Such an inventory can change our entire life perception. Sometimes, we are succeeding at life, but tell ourselves we are losing. We fail to have the joy of our success because we do not see it, even if it is right in front of our eyes.

SANE INVENTORY

To know how to live in the now, we must know who we are and what we have in the now. Because we have a tendency to survive and not thrive, we often are ignorant of where we actually are at the present time. This includes our inner and outer realities. Naïve views based on misconceptions are seldom accurate. This is why we need to take inventory and create systems to maintain an accurate view of our life.

It is important to know who we were in the past, but also who we are in the present. Some of us are living in the glory of past victories and not seeing the present erosion of our lives. Others, stinging from past defeats, are unable to see the tide has turned and their present life is filled with wonderful blessings. People rarely take the time to smell the proverbial roses.

Our goal is to realistically know our strengths and our weaknesses. To know the present reality is the aim. Future goals can only be set if we know our starting point. Therefore, we must honestly decide we want to know everything we can about our present state. To succeed at life is the state of being complete, entire, and balanced. Unity among all the parts of our life gives us a comprehensive, healthy effectiveness in our daily living. To the degree we have a sense of having a healthy and secure life, loving and being loved, experience healthy laughter, feel we are learning more about ultimate reality, and are leaving a legacy that matters; we experience a sense that we are succeeding at life.

Without knowledge of our current condition we cannot inform ourselves how far we have to go to reach the goals we feel we should reach to effectively be living life to its full potential. Being in touch with the present is a critical aspect of being healthy and complete as a person. Living in the present is the only way to bring our full energy and focus to bear on the issues, potentials, and problems of our lives. To be fully engaged, we must be fully awake to the present moment.

To take inventory we must be willing to take stock of all the various aspects of our life. This will include all spheres of our life. From this inventory, we will be in a position to evaluate our current state of being. We must also seek to create a system where we will systematically update this inventory every year; so that we can continue to get feedback on where we are and the direction we are headed.

What type of inventories do we need to take? The following inventories are tools to help you get a clear accounting of your current position.

1. Life and Security
2. Loving and Being Loved
3. Laughing and Fun
4. Learning and Living with Truth
5. Leaving an Honorable Legacy

First Inventory: Life and Security

Mark those which are true[17]

1. I have had a complete physical exam in the past two years.

2. I exercise on a regular basis.

3. I am aware of physical and/or emotional problems or conditions I

have. I am taking responsible steps in having these treated by

professionals.

4. I am happy with my level of energy.

---

[17] It is obvious if you lie on this inventory to appear better than you are, the only person you are lying to is yourself. For this exercise to work you must be totally honest and transparent with yourself.

5. I do not use illegal drugs, abuse prescribed medications, or become intoxicated.

6. I do not live a rushed life.

7. I enjoy my work and know when to stop.

8. I have a responsible diet.

9. I keep my teeth and gums healthy and see a dentist every six months.

10. I have a well planned and balanced schedule that reflects my values.

11. I regularly balance my checkbook.

12. I spend less than I make.

13. I plan to save.

14. I have a budget.

15. I am adequately insured.

16. I have a financial plan for my life.

17. I have paid my taxes.

18. I pay my bills on time.

19. I am not worried or anxious about my debts.

20. I have medical insurance.

Total positive answers _____

Second Inventory: Loving and Being Loved

Mark those that are true

1. I tell the significant people in my life I love them on a regular basis.

2. I am on good speaking terms with my family members.

3. I am good at communicating my thoughts and feelings.

4. I respect and honor those with whom I work.

5. I feel respected and honored by those with whom I work.

6. I have a close circle of friends with whom I am emotionally intimate.

7. I am emotionally intimate with my family.

8. I value people not for what they can do for me, but simply for who they are.

9. I am a person of my word and keep my promises.

10. The significant people in my life tell me they love me on a regular basis.

11. I do not use dirty fighting techniques when I get into a conflict.

12. I am good at listening to the needs of others.

13. I am open to compromise in making decisions

14. I do not feel rejected when my "solutions" are rejected.

15. I don't isolate when I am mad to make others feel bad for upsetting me.

16. I have control of my temper.

17. I can value my opinions and others opinions at the same time.

18. I do not abuse people with my words or actions.

19. The significant people in my life seek out fellowship with me.

20. I feel loved by God and love God.

Total positive answers _____

Third Inventory: Laughing and Fun

Mark those that are true

1. I have a healthy laugh on a regular basis.

2. I know how to provide myself a good time without moral compromise.

3. I know my favorite foods and eat them often.

4. I make time for my hobbies.

5. I purposely do things that will give me joy daily.

6. I know how to take "mini vacations" during the day to reduce stress.

7. I don't take myself too seriously.

8. I take time to remember what is going right.

9. I know how to joke around in a healthy way without harming others.

10. I take time off work and have one full day of rest each week.

11. I take vacations.

12. When I am sick, I stay home and rest.

13. I have a list of activities I want to do before I die that I think would be fun.

14. I know how to relax when on vacation.

15. I allow myself time as an adult to "play".

16. I purposely expose myself to things that I find beautiful.

17. I know how to rejoice when other people are happy.

18. I watch some movies or other entertainment just to make me feel good.

19. I can "treat" myself when I need to lift my spirits.

20. I know how to enjoy God in times of private and public worship.

Total positive answers _____

Fourth Inventory: Learning and Living Truth

Mark those that are true

1. I read significant books on a regular basis.

2. I have significant conversations with others in the search for truth.

3. I have changed something I did because I came to believe there was a better way.

4. I listen to people lecture on important topics.

5. I take classes and attend groups to increase my understanding.

6. I evaluate my behaviors to see if they are consistent with my values.

7. I have written out my values.

8. I don't allow television to eat up all my free time.

9. I look for significant television shows to watch that will help me think.

10. I seek to watch some movies just to challenge me to think

11. I research things on the internet or at the public library.

12. I am not satisfied with what I currently know.

13. I am open to changing my mind if new evidence is presented.

14. I try to live consistent with my beliefs and values.

15. Hypocrisy bothers me.

16. I spend time writing out my thoughts about life in a journal.

17. I like to listen to others express their viewpoints since from this I may learn.

18. I am reading the Bible or some other significant literature about God.

19. I do not want to be mislead about reality.

20. I love the truth.

Total positive answers _____

Fifth Inventory: Leaving an Honorable Legacy

Mark those that are true

1. In my will I am leaving some of my resources to make the future better.

2. I am living today the way I want people to remember me at my funeral.

3. I have a list of meaningful acts that I want to accomplish before I die.

4. I am investing in younger people so that what I have learned will be passed on.

5. I am committed to helping charities so that others will be helped by them.

6. I have a list of people I need to reconcile with before I die.

7. I have enough insurance to pay off all my debts.

8. I have provided for my dependents after I die.

9. I have written up my "final words" for all the members of my family.

10. I am working to finish what I believe is God's will for my life before I die.

11. I care about leaving the world a better place then when I arrived.

12. I keep myself concerned about culture and the direction of society.

13. I would be willing to die in order to make the world more just.

14. I care about the poor and needy.

15. There is more to life than personal happiness and affluence.

16. I think the world has become overly materialistic.

17. I write my political leaders and urge them to take right actions.

18. I express my strongest beliefs with conviction.

19. I am willing to lose money in order to be honest.

20. I value moral integrity.

Total positive answers _____

Use these inventories to see where you stand at the present moment in your quest towards succeeding at life. You can eliminate any questions you honestly do think do not apply to you and replace them with ones that are relevant. There are a total of 100 statements here. Total up the number of "yes" answers to these questions that apply and give yourself a "success at life" score.

My Succeeding at Life Score is _____

How do you feel about that score? Could you make it better?

How?

STABLE EVALUATON

Now that you have taken an inventory of your present condition, it is time to examine this data with a stable and clear evaluation. Perhaps you would like to add some items to each of the categories and remove some of those provided. This is a great thing to do. The more personal and realistic these inventories are the better.

As you look over your answers, in which of the five areas of life are you the strongest? Which are the weakest areas in your life?

1. Life and Security   _____
2. Loving and Being Loved   _____
3. Laughing and Fun   _____
4. Learning and Living Truth _____
5. Leaving an Honorable Legacy _____

What do your scores reveal about you? Do they suggest where you need to put in your greatest effort to find wholeness for your heart?

Let us imagine you had a very close friend who had the scores you had on these inventories. What words of encouragement and advice would you give your friend? Imagine he/she has shared his/her scores with you and is honestly seeking your most transparent feedback.

What I would tell my best friend based on the inventories I took?

_____

_____

_____

_____

_____

_____

_____

_____

_____

_____

_____

_____

_____

_____

_____

_____

_____

_____

_____

_____

Do you think the inventories accurately reflect your most cherished values? What was the most encouraging aspect of what the inventories revealed to you? Evaluation is all about asking yourself questions. Ponder deeply where you are at the present moment and identify any areas where you think you may want to change.

KEY THINGS I WOULD LIKE TO CHANGE

_____

_____

_____

_____

_____

_____

_____

Remember, as you think about your inventories, to avoid "black and white" thinking. On the one hand be challenged and on the other be encouraged. This is the only evaluation that is balanced and realistic.

SPIRITUAL RESOURCES

One of the most important inventories we can take is one that deals with morality and spirituality. The following is a moral inventory which can help us get a sense of how we are doing in the areas of spirituality and ethics. Take time to fill it out to provide you with an honest evaluation of your moral/spiritual state.

Moral Value	Scale of Obedience				
	Not at all	Not very	No Opinion	Some-what	Extremely
I love and serve God	1	2	3	4	5
I love and serve people	1	2	3	4	5
I love myself and maintain a healthy lifestyle	1	2	3	4	5
I invest time in private and public worship	1	2	3	4	5
I speak kindly to people and do not curse	1	2	3	4	5
I speak with respect about those in authority	1	2	3	4	5
I obey ethical commands made by those in authority at work and in society	1	2	3	4	5
I try my best when I work	1	2	3	4	5
I rest one day a week to renew my strength	1	2	3	4	5
I do not waste money on things I do not need	1	2	3	4	5
I do not take what belongs to another	1	2	3	4	5
I listen to my spouse with respect	1	2	3	4	5

Moral Value	Scale of Obedience				
	Not at all	Not very	No Opinion	Some-what	Extremely
I avoid pornography	1	2	3	4	5
I listen to my children	1	2	3	4	5
I seek to be sexually pure	1	2	3	4	5
I am content with what I own	1	2	3	4	5
I tell the truth even when it is hard	1	2	3	4	5
I am patient	1	2	3	4	5
I exercise self control and do not lose my temper	1	2	3	4	5
I tell my spouse I love them	1	2	3	4	5
I tell my children I love them	1	2	3	4	5
I am willing to suffer for doing the right thing	1	2	3	4	5

I give time and money to help those in need	1	2	3	4	5

Of course, there is more to spirituality and morality than an inventory. We may feel guilty after taking this inventory. Feeling appropriate guilt is sometimes realistic. But, once we have come to see we have fallen short of God's ideal for our lives, what do we do then? The answer to this is given by the disciple John, who was the best friend of Jesus.

> *"This is real love. It is not that we loved God, but that He loved us and sent his Son as a sacrifice to take away our sins."* 1 John 4:10 NLT

Therefore, we should not see God as a taker, but a giver. It is His desire for us to be completely forgiven and ready to succeed at life. This is why He sent Jesus Christ to die for our sins.

How then can spirituality help us on a daily basis? One of the present realities is the potential for the presence, peace, and power of God to add vitality and strength to our practical lives. If we properly understand spirituality, we gain a moment by moment opportunity to succeed at life. To gain the presence, peace, and power of God requires we use spiritual "rituals", "disciplines", or "practices" which act as "means of grace" through which our experience of the divine comes into our lives.

What spiritual practices will work to keep you renewed? This is a very personal question, but worth pondering. Some basic ones that have been useful to many people are:

- Experimenting with at least fifteen minutes of quiet prayer and a meditation where we seek truth on a regular basis is vital. Having a book of inspirational thoughts and a moment to journal is great. The book *Spiritual Classics* by Richard J. Foster and Emilie Griffin is a good start.

- In the "24/7" rat race of our society, God calls us to rest one day a week. Sabbath can be a vital addition to keep our present in a sane, stable, and spiritual space. This day should be a day of self nurture, reflection, seeking inspiration, and asking ourselves the big questions of life. Having a time for public and private worship can help us find inner strength.

In the appendix on "Matters of Faith," I have provided resources for spiritual rituals we can add to the enthusiasm of our lives. If you have an interest in deepening your knowledge of this area then it would be a good idea to read that appendix now.

Where do you find your enthusiasm? To be enthusiastic is to be literally "filled with God." By having union and communion with the living God on a regular basis, we can experience sanity and stability. The original divine plan for our lives was to feel alive and secure as we fellowship with Him.

God is love and we must know He loves us and that we love Him. God's desire is to fill us with His joy and laughter, while teaching us the whole essence of truth. His design for humanity is to live significant lives. As we seek to succeed at life, we must ultimately recognize this can only take place by being reconciled to God through faith in Jesus Christ. We will then experience a dynamic, real, mature, balanced, intelligent, and practical life in Him.

Today is a great day to be reconciled to God. To have true union with God allows us to return to His original plan for us to succeed at life. This is done by deciding to believe Jesus Christ is the unique incarnation[18] of deity, ask Him to forgive your sins and trust Him to teach you the truth and guide you in the decisions of life.

You may find the following prayer helpful in moving in the direction of knowing and trusting Jesus:

"Father, I know that I have broken your moral standards and this unethical behavior on my part has separated me from you. I am truly sorry, and now I want to turn away from insanity, instability, and selfishness and return to you. Please forgive me, and help me to stop loving insane, abusive, self centered and chaotic behaviors. I believe that Jesus Christ, the incarnation of God, died for my sins, was resurrected from the dead, is alive, and hears my prayer. I invite Jesus to become the Lord of my life, to rule and reign in my heart from this day forward. Please send your Holy Spirit to help me

---

[18] For a book that outlines clearly how to do this I would recommend *The Answer* by Randy Pope

strive to be sane, stable, and spiritual for the rest of
my life. In Jesus' name I pray, Amen."

This prayer will not fix everything. As we said in the beginning, there are people who are Christians who are not succeeding at life. However, taking this initial step is a critical one for those who want to succeed at life. It lays a good foundation towards becoming sane, stable, and spiritual.

Now some of you may have intellectual doubts about faith and Christ. To have faith in Jesus Christ one must first intellectually accept what is taught about him is true. A great book to use to think about this is; Lee Strobel's *The Case for Christ: A Journalist's Personal Investigation of the Evidence for Jesus* and Tim Keller's book *The Reason For God: Belief in an Age of Skepticism*. I think investigating the truthfulness of the claims of Jesus of Nazareth is worth the effort because faith in Him opens the door for a life of grace, love, forgiveness, and encouragement.

Chapter three Exercises

1. List the values and principles that you currently believe in strongly?

2. What are your key roles at the present time? (For example: spouse, business owner, church member, parent, union representative) List each of your roles and describe how you would define this role in your life at the present time. Evaluate the role's importance on a scale from 1 to 10 with 10 being extremely important

3. What is the best thing about your present life?

Journal for Chapter Three

What thoughts, feelings, impressions, questions, or musings came through this chapter?

_____

_____

_____

_____

_____

_____

_____

_____

_____

_____

_____

_____

_____

_____

_____

_____

_____

_____

_____

_____

_____

_____

_____

_____

_____

_____

_____

_____

_____

_____

_____

"One can never consent to creep

when one feels an impulse to soar"

Helen Keller

Chapter Four – Preferred Future

MAIN THOUGHT:

It is vital for our personal growth towards succeeding at life, that we have a well defined, envisioned, evaluated, and processed preferred future. If we are totally satisfied with where we are at the present time, it is unlikely we will work hard to change into someone better.

Opening Exercise:

Think about getting into a time machine, as was imagined by H.G. Wells. You are about to take a trip to the future. You arrive in the same room you are currently in now. In that room, you meet your future self, the person you will be in ten years. At first both of you are shocked. But, once you explain the time travel, your future self calms down and ask you to sit down. Imagine your future self over the last ten years has diligently attempted to fully develop into a sane, stable, and spiritual person inwardly and outwardly. What differences do you notice between this person and you? Remember, you imagined you had made it your top priority to fully develop inner self control, live a balanced life, and fulfill your divine destiny. Think about what questions you would like to ask your future self. What advice do you imagine your future self giving you? Now imagine getting back into the time machine and returning to the present. What are your feelings? What thoughts do you have? Are you motivated to do anything different?

Basic Thoughts:

Life is a voyage. We begin by leaving the safe harbor of our mother's womb. After being trained in the skills of a life mariner in our home of origin, we are called to captain our ship through the ocean of life so we will reach a specific destination. However skilled we are at sailing and maintaining the ship, the purpose of the journey is to arrive at a destination. A ship without a destination is lost. A life without a destination is adrift. A critical step in succeeding at life is to define clearly what we believe to be our destination in life. Each person has a unique destination.

Once we have processed the past and evaluated the present, we are ready to envision the future. Knowing where we are in life gives us a starting point for navigating the course to where we are headed. Without a well defined preferred future, it is impossible to set goals or to evaluate our effectiveness.

God has given each person an ideal life purpose. There are no insignificant people and no irrelevant places. Every person and every place is significant. The greatest leaders would be nothing without loyal followers. Each of us is called to fit into the whole. You have a purpose for your life.

When a person fulfills his or her ideal life purpose and potential he has left a great legacy to human history. When we are moving in the direction of our life purpose, we have direction, intentionality, and connectedness. When we fail to move in the direction of fulfilling this ideal life purpose we feel lost and lacking focus. If we end up totally missing our life purpose, then we fail to leave a fulfilled legacy. It is vital we define our preferred future.

The basic tool we use to define this ideal life purpose is the construction of a life mission statement. Through a process of careful self examination we answer questions about what we were created to accomplish. At times, we may not know the ultimate destination and only have a clear vision of the next stop along the road. But this is enough to give us immediate direction today.

This mission statement will help us settle on our direction. It allows us to make decisions in light of our long term goals, rather than immediate feelings and temptations. Having a clear life mission statement allows us to live more consistently with our ideals and persevere in doing what is right during difficult times.

Illustration of the Principle:

There was a woman who had dedicated her life to business. It had gone through many different cycles. Some of the cycles had proven very profitable. Some had been very difficult and stress producing. Her focus and dedication to her work put strains on her marriage and relationship with her children. Her husband demanded she reevaluate her priorities because their relationship went up and down with the business cycles. He insisted she make some immediate changes, but she refused saying, "You just don't understand my business!" He also felt their children were being neglected in her "holy quest" for business success. She refused to get counseling. He divorced her because he felt rejected, abandoned, and manipulated by her business "love affair".

At first, this did not seem to slow her down. After a telephone conversation when he seemed open to reconciliation, she saw this might be a second and only chance. She began seeing a life coach.

Her greatest struggle was her entire existence was defined within the framework of her business. As she developed a statement reflecting where she currently was in her life, she said "I am the leader of my company so that I can prove that I am a success". When the life coach asked her to consider if this statement satisfied the deepest part of her being as an ideal life purpose statement, it took her only a moment to realize it really fell short of what she wanted to be. It was hard for her to imagine herself not living by that statement, since it had defined her for so long. But through a process of personal reflection and hearing the words actually spoken, she was positive they fell short.

As the life coach worked with her over a period of time and asked her to define her values, she began to see part of her problem was she had never fully defined "success". She believed it only had to do with the bottom line. She recognized she felt her family would love her more in direct proportion to the amount of money she made. At the end of the process, she had written a life purpose statement which expressed where she really wanted to be in her life. It read, "I am a hardworking and faithful person who wants to express creativity through my work and my relationships with my family." This led her to give up her own company that was at a historic low cycle and become a dynamic team member of a company where her creative abilities would be used without overloading her. For the first time in a couple of decades, this allowed her to start spending time with her family. Today, she is happier and more balanced than at any other time in her entire life.

SANE ALTERNATIVES

So how do you begin to find your "ideal life purpose?" At first glance, this seems very hard to really do. How can a person know for sure what her destination is supposed to be? What are the possible options you have? How do you really do this?

To begin, sit down with a journal book and start to list every future you think possible. At this stage, do not evaluate which of these futures are better or worse than others. List possibilities of what you believe you could do or would like to do. Allow your mind to be totally free during this time.

Once you have this list, there are a couple of different ways to better define your purpose for living. One of them is provided by Dietrich Bonhoeffer, a Lutheran pastor executed by the Nazis because of his opposition to Adolph Hitler. He suggested we live our lives backwards to live purposeful lives. What he meant by this is to imagine we are already standing before the Judgment Seat of God. Then, make every decision based on how we would like to see our life presented before God for judgment. If in our mind a decision would be a bad choice to report to God on Judgment Day, then it is a bad choice to make today.

This is a good reality check, since we must give an answer to God for everything we do in this life. The image Pastor Bonhoeffer had was before we make a decision, we should mentally take it through this process. This idea can be broadened by figuratively taking the list of alternative futures before the Judgment Seat of Christ. Which of them do I feel most pleases God? Why do I feel one alternative future is more pleasing to God than another? Is my reasoning valid and mature?

I could take these thoughts to my life coach or other trusted advisors to see what they thought about my process. They should not attempt to define my life purpose, but simply ask me clarifying questions to help me think more clearly. This is one way we can obtain the general outline of our life purpose.

Another method has been suggested by Stephen Covey author of the *Seven Habits of Highly Effective People.* Dr. Covey suggests we imagine our funeral and have every important person in our lives give a eulogy. What do we want them to say about us? What do we want them to say we accomplished? We can also imagine different eulogies based upon our choosing different preferred futures. Which of these eulogies most satisfies our spirit? Why is one preferred future better than another when judged from the viewpoint of our death and funeral?

Both of these exercises are helpful in us developing the life vision statement for our lives. A life vision statement is what we want our life to be all about. It can be one sentence or one paragraph. In addition, we need to have a mission statement that will be a longer and more detailed summary of what we want to live for and the direction we are called to take. The formation of our life vision statement and mission statement are a critical part of our developing a concrete definition of our preferred future. This should be an issue of sincere prayer as we attempt to discover God's preferred future for our lives.

It is important we make our life vision statement reflect our having 100% control as much as possible. We want to proactively seek our purpose. This can only happen if we define our vision within the confines of what we have control over. This implies our vision cannot have control over others or outside circumstances. In some cases, we may have to presuppose some things. To this degree, our plans must always be flexible.

Examples of proactive life vision statements would be:

> I desire to provide care for hurting people so that I may express the love of Christ to people in need.
> I desire to be a loving person so that I may provide my family an opportunity to know compassion and care in their lives.
> I desire to be a logical and systematic thinker who wants to offer the fruits of my writing and my family wise guidance in making decisions.
> I desire to be a lover of hard work and provide quality service to others and my family.
> I desire to be a disciple of Jesus and to live by the principles of the Sermon on the Mount so that I may reflect his life to my family, friends, and culture.

Examples of reactive life vision statements would be:

> I desire to provide care for hurting people knowing that they will recover from their hurts if I do this correctly.
> I desire to be a loving person so that my family will know that I have compassion and care for them and will return love to me.

> I desire to be a logical and systematic thinker who will correct the wrong thinking of the world through my writings and make my family wisely decide in every situation.
> I am a lover of hard work so that others will appreciate the high quality of work I produce and will have a good income from my labor.
> I am a disciple of Jesus Christ and desire to live by the principles of the Sermon on the Mount, so that I will bring about transformation in my family, friends, and culture.

We must strive to make our vision statements proactive and not reactive if they are to be realistic.

One of the struggles of making a life vision statement is to summarize the entire direction of our lives in a very broad statement. It is hard for a vision statement not be become "reductionist" since one particular focus of our life may be the ultimate concern we have and is the focus for our activities. In order to avoid this, it is sometimes better to formulate a partial vision statement for the various aspects and roles of our lives. Once we have written out these partial vision statements, it can be easier to write a broad statement that reflects our genuine desires.

The other question we must ask ourselves is what is at the center of all our other desires? We can see this in the following illustration.

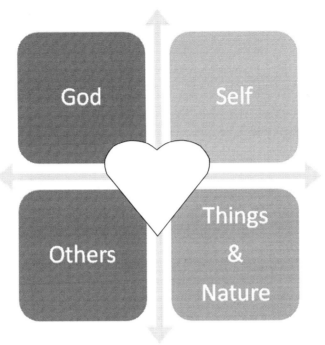

We can do many things with this chart. We could rate each area on a scale from one to ten with ten being most important and one being the least important. We may even decide we want to eliminate one or more boxes in the matrix. The key here is to use this illustration to help us clarify our preferred future.

Our life vision statement is represented by the heart in the chart. This is the "prime directive" for our lives and gives direction in every aspect of our lives. It is this "prime directive" we are attempting to discover, evaluate, affirm, or replace. We may find that our "prime directive" has been too limiting or causing us to lack wholeness in our lives.
Write out Partial Vision Statements:

1.   The Spiritual Vision: I desire...

_____

_____

2.   The Physical: I desire...

_____

3.   The Career Vision: I desire...

_____

_____

4.   The Financial Vision: I desire...

_____

_____

5.   The Health Vision: I desire...

_____

_____

6.   The Friend Vision: I desire...

_____

_____

7.   The Family Vision: I desire...

_____

_____

8.   The Romance Vision: I desire...

_____

_____

9.   The Personal Growth Vision: I desire...

_____

10.   The Fun Vision: I desire...

_____

_____

_____

Look at your desires in all ten areas. Is there some unifying theme, value, principle, belief, commitment, feeling, or outlook that unites all ten?   Even if it is below the surface, is there something perhaps only you can see that really unites all of the other ten vision statements in your innermost self?
Attempt to write down here your heart vision or life vision statement.

My heart vision statement I desire ….

What are your impressions about what you have written? Does this seem real to you? Does this reflect who you really are or who you want to become?   How do you feel about this vision statement? Does it feel right to you? Does it inspire you? Do you feel enthusiastic about seeking it to become reality? How do you think it should be changed? How would you modify or clarify it?

It is alright to take your time on these statements. They are going to provide the definition of your destination in life. You want to make sure they represent what you believe to be the divine purpose and plan that is unique for you.

God has interest in every human activity. There are no little people or little places to Him. What seems to be a small success to one person is no less significant than what appears to be a grander plan. The key here is to be faithful to who we are. From the one who has been given little, then little will be required; but to the one who has been given much, then much will be required. One important thing is that you have in clear conscience and right thinking attempted prayerfully to understand God's purpose for you to succeed at life.

Once you have written your life vision statements and have attempted to define your heart vision statement you are ready to begin working on developing your mission statement. The mission statement sets forth in greater detail not only what you hope to see happen in your life, but how you hope to see it accomplished. The mission statement gives more color and detail to your vision. This helps solidify it and make it more real to you.

This mission statement should still be seen as a broad summary and not a detailed listing of goals. That will come later as you begin the process of prioritization. For the moment, you should write out a mission statement no longer than one page that provides more depth and understanding to your life vision statement. In many ways, a mission statement could be described as an expanded definition of your life vision statement. I am providing my own life vision and mission statements to help you be able to form your own. Remember, your statements must be totally unique to you even as mine are totally unique to me.

Thoughts

_____

_____

_____

_____

_____

_____

_____

An Example of a Life Vision And Mission Statement

<u>My Life Vision Statement</u>

I desire to be an emotionally healthy disciple of Jesus the Messiah who is fully engaged and devoted to Him as my personal prophet, priest, and king. I believe that discipleship to Messiah Jesus will bring spiritual healing and wholeness to my core personality. I hope that this inner healing and harmony of my soul will allow me to love my family, care for hurting people, and encourage peace in and among the people I influence. I want to be a peacemaker and promote peace in hearts and homes.

<u>My Mission Statement:</u>

I desire to be an emotionally healthy disciple of Jesus the Messiah by living by the principles of the Sermon on the Mount and using spiritual disciplines on a daily basis.

I desire to be in mystical union and communion with Jesus the Messiah through private and public worship experiences.

I desire to have a strong intellectual reason for my faith in Messiah Jesus.

I desire to be a hearer and doer of God's Word.

I desire to show unconditional mercy and grace to others as God has poured out His mercy and grace upon me in Messiah Jesus.

I desire to show my love to my wife and children in concrete and tangible ways.

I desire to help others find healing of their hearts and homes by teaching, counseling, coaching, pastoring, facilitating small groups, directing spiritual retreats, and encouraging an emotionally healthy church.

I desire to have the comfort I have received concerning the pain that I have experienced in my life become a means of bringing comfort to other hurting people for generations after I die.

I desire to demonstrate before the watching world that Christians can be rational, kind, understanding, and human.

I desire to enjoy Sabbath rest and relax in the midst of a productive life.

While the process of defining our preferred futures may take many months, it is well worth the effort! In this particular activity hiring, a "life coach" can be well worth the investment. Life coaches are people whose entire job description is to assist others to close the gap between where they are and where they want to go. Unlike counselors whose primary focus is on the past, a life coach's aim is to help one reach the preferred future one thinks is best for him. Living Water Life Coaching is available to help those who may desire a life coach. There are a growing number of qualified life coaches around the country able to assist people in this process. The important thing is to take the time to develop a sane evaluation of your future and apply the process needed to head in the right direction.

STABLE CONSIDERATIONS

All of this work will do little good if you put down your life vision on a piece of paper and stuff it in a drawer to be forgotten. Many times, we find ourselves able to focus for short periods of time on critical issues like life vision statements, but all too quickly they yield to the "tyranny of the urgent". Many individuals and organizations have gone through the blood, sweat, and tears of carefully framing a vision statement, only to have it end up in the trash heap of hurry and habit. What can we do to prevent this from happening?

We must understand how positive and deliberate change takes place in our lives. We must first have a vision. Following the vision we must make a strong, conscious, and committed choice to do what it takes to bring our vision into the real world. We return to the proactive principle, we must accept the responsibility to make our vision a reality. Once we have truly intended to make the vision reality, it simply is a matter of finding the right methods. Having the right methods is critical. Without them the best of intentions only leads to frustration. In the next chapter, we will be discussing more about methods of bringing our life vision or heart vision into reality.

However, the key here is we must intentionally not allow our written vision to be forgotten; but put it on our computer screens, our refrigerators, or anywhere we will see it. The first part of true intention is to regularly read and review it. We may revise it. That is fine. Anything that keeps it alive and growing, focuses our activities.

We can also look at our current use of time. We need to make a list of all our regularly scheduled events, meetings, or actions. Write next to them, "vision consistent" or "inconsistent". We can also add things we should have on our list that would be "vision consistent", but are not now on our schedule. At this point, we could combine these lists and make one "vision consistent". This will help us as we prioritize our lives in the next section.

For those activities I have labeled "inconsistent"; I need to rate each of them on a scale from one to ten, ten being highly committed to doing them and one being minimally committed. If I have an action labeled "inconsistent" on a level between eight and ten, then I need to ask what value in my life this behavior represents. Perhaps, I am denying part of who I am and my vision statement is incomplete. For the others, I need to write out a plan of how I will move these out of my schedule. Our life is measured in time. We are limited to 168 hours a week. The more time we give to doing things not consistent with our vision, the less likely our

vision will be accomplished. We will deal with this in more depth in the next chapter, but these exercises are a good process to help harmonize our outward life with our inward reality.

The main way to stabilize our life vision is to consciously, formally, and concretely commit to keeping your vision in front of you and sincerely choose to make your vision a reality. If you do this, and keep this choice before you for the next 90 days, all you need is the right methods for your heart vision to become your lifestyle.

Thoughts

_____

_____

_____

_____

_____

_____

Vision Consistent and Inconsistent chart

Activities	Consistent	Inconsistent	How to get rid of or add

SPIRITUAL DIRECTION

The actual process of choosing a life vision should be done with the input of our spiritual directors, leaders, and clergy. At our core we are spiritual beings and therefore, we must be sure what we discern as our prime direction lines up with who we are at a spiritual level. This will avoid a conflict between what we may see as "God's will" and "our will". It is better to face this problem and not deny its reality.

One of the key issues is to understand God is not the universal "kill joy". His main job is not to keep people from having fun. God through his commandments warns people of harmful activities. However, He is the source of joy. God rejoices when we have healthy joy and happiness. If we find the divine purpose for our life, we will also find the deepest well of the most profound joy.

God is the maker of all of life. He has never accepted the secular vs. spiritual separation found in our society. All of life... relationships, vocation, hobbies, science, and art are all of interest to God. He is calling people to be fully engaged in every aspect of life. God is not only focused on what happens in religious institutions! God is interested in vocations, relationships, families, and cultures as much as He is interested in things we see as "religious". Because of this, being called by God to do something does not mean we have to join some religious organization and only be involved in "religious" things. Instead, we need to see God's interest in the everyday reality of our lives and in every aspect of our existence.

This does not mean our life vision may not require us to suffer. Like mothers who must go through pregnancy to give birth, we may go through times of difficulty and in order to "give birth" into reality the visions God has for us to accomplish in our lives. The pain is not due to any lack of love on God's part. God's own vision of the Kingdom of God on earth could not be "birthed" without the suffering of Messiah Jesus on the cross. The most valuable visions always cost us; but are always worth the sacrifices once they have been born.

Therefore do not attempt to hide this process from God or be afraid of his involvement. Instead, seek His help in prayer and meditation. Ask Him to help you to use the tools provided in this chapter towards a clearer understanding of His will for your life. Remember, God's will is not that everyone should be a missionary in some dark and terrible place! He invites some people to become astronauts, bakers, builders, and bank tellers. God's interests are as broad as human creativity and skill. He is the Maker of them and rejoices when gifts are used. A healthy spirituality has a very broad understanding of God's intentions. Don't think God is attempting to limit you. Remember, He is without limits!

SUMMARY

Dealing with our past and evaluating our present has brought us to a great position for seeking our preferred future. Inner harmony comes when our outside matches what we are inside. As we define the gap between who we are and where we are and who we want to be and where we want to go, we will now clearly navigate the seas of life and sail our way to our most desired destiny. We are actively in the process of succeeding at life.

Chapter Four Exercises

1. Set aside a weekend to define your preferred vision. Go to a place where you will be able to think, write, process, relax, and have fun. Turn off your cell phone for a couple of days and write down on paper or on a computer the plan for the rest of your life.

2. What do you believe will be the greatest obstacles to living your life vision? List them here. Then by each obstacle plan a way to overcome it.

3. What is the most exciting part of defining and having a life vision?

Journal for Chapter Four

What thoughts and feelings are you having after reading this chapter?

_____

_____

_____

_____

_____

_____

_____

_____

_____

_____

_____

_____

_____

_____

_____

_____

_____

_____

_____

The only way to know what is a priority is to determine which preferred future we are aiming toward. If my preferred future is to live my life memorizing the plots of soap operas, then watching hours of television in the afternoon is a priority. But if my preferred future is to gain self control, then making time to attend my weekly accountability meeting is a priority. Priorities are decisions about what is important based on values, principles, and vision. Until we are aware of our vision, we will not have proper priorities but instead those motivated by our desire to seek out immediate and superficial pleasure.

Success is also determined by vision. Success for Mother Teresa was different than for Bill Gates. Only when we know what our life vision is can we determine if we are successful or unsuccessful in fulfilling it.

Chapter Five – Priorities for Success

MAIN PURPOSE:

To outline the methods to organize our lifestyle so we will begin to invest our minutes, hours, days, weeks, and months towards inward and outward harmony of our values and actions. This is succeeding at life!

OPENING EXERCISE:

Imagine you had a totally open schedule for the next year. You were free to do whatever you wanted for the next 52 weeks. What would you do with this time? What do you think would be the most profitable use of your time? Would this alter any of your current priorities? Would you put back into your schedule what you are currently doing? Why or why not?

Basic thoughts:

Our journey has brought us to the point of giving birth to a new lifestyle. This is going to be YOUR NEW LIFE STYLE! This lifestyle will bring your life into harmony with your deepest values, beliefs and desires. Rather than being fragmented, you will move in the direction of wholeness; inwardly and outwardly. Personal peace is experienced to the degree our outer world matches our deepest inner desires. You have laid the foundation for this last step. There is nothing to keep you from progressively and significantly framing your life into a healthy and whole structure so you can succeed at life.

Actually making the changes in priorities will help overcome obstacles from ingrained habits and fear of disapproval. You will likely make the changes gradually and deal with certain set realities. You will have to determine how much you want to risk in bringing about change. Remember, as long as your direction is on course, time is your friend. As long as your direction is right and your intention is firm, over time you can systematically bring about significant change. We can plan gradual and substantial change. We have the power to choose holistic lives instead of a fragmented existence. We can succeed at life.

ILLLUSTRATION OF THE PRINCIPLE:

There was a business owner who lived a life of great stress and "success". He had over 3000 customers and 20 employees. He was the sole salesperson for his company and the only person in management. He had a very good income, but no time to enjoy it. His health was suffering due to stress-related illness. He was seldom home, but his family had stopped complaining out of exasperation. He did not have any sense of fulfillment, even though he had a great business.

The businessman decided to have a consultant come in to provide insight into how life could be made easier. On the day the consultant arrived he found the business owner answering phone calls and interacting with his employees by radio. The consultant observed the owner, and looked through computer reports on the company. The consultant had told him the first day all he would do is observe. There really was very little time to talk, since the owner was in an unending series of crisis. His lunch was spent running around on sales calls. In the afternoon he was interacting with customers and employees. After about ten straight, nonstop hours the owner was ready to meet with the consultant. As they walked into the office the business owner's desk was filled with papers he had not been able to get to because he had been on the phone all day.

The owner apologized for the mess. He started the conversation with a grin, "Well as you can see we are really busy. Hardly time to breath." The consultant laughed, "I was concerned for a while there you might actually forget to do that." The owner sat back in his chair with one eye on the pile of papers crying out for his attention. He said, "Well, any ideas about how to make things better?" The consultant replied, "I noticed you are answering your own phone…" Before he could finish his sentence, the owner was leaning forward and retorted in a defensive voice, " Now you have to understand, that keeps me at the center of everything, I can talk to the customers and keep tabs on my people. That is the center of the storm and no one but me can do it. Plus, I am saving money on a dispatcher and receptionist." The consultant took a moment to think about what had been said. Then he replied; "Well, you certainly are right no one can do it the way you can. But, I don't think you are saving money on a dispatcher and receptionist. In fact, I think you have the best paid dispatcher and receptionist in the world." The owner looked puzzled and said, "What do you mean?" The consultant replied, "Well, from looking at your financials and figuring the hours you spend in that seat, I would estimate you are paying $100,000 to get the job of dispatching done and that does not even calculate the lost opportunities for sales. My guess is you are spending about $200,000 a year for that position. The owner looked stunned. He could see the consultant was right. This business insight opened him up to the idea he really had to change what he was doing. The question was, could he really control his time and not try to control everything else.

Within the next few weeks, he had hired a dispatcher receptionist and an office manager. The consultant interviewed him about his values, desires, and dreams. He suggested by changing the structure of his business and personal time, the door would open to achieving what the owner really wanted.

The consultant had him organize his time so 80% was out on the road making sales calls and talking to customers. That is what the owner loved. It is what he had done to build the company in the beginning. He hated the office and the administrative side. Being with customers face to face and selling is what made a day at work "fun" for him.

The owner had the liberty to talk with his employees by radio from his car and could respond to any technical problems the dispatcher or manager could not handle. In about six months, it was rare for that to happen. He now had time to have lunch with his wife and went home earlier. His family relationships improved. He began living the life he always wanted, but just could not find the time. His business doubled its income that year due to the extra time he spent on sales and improvements made by the office manager. By changing his schedule to reflect what he really wanted, he had given more time for family, increased his involvement in church, enjoyed planned times of recreation, had improved health due to less stress, and had greater financial security. All this was due to evaluating his priorities. This was the key to his succeeding at life.

SANE PROCESS

How can we change what we do? How do we align our daily schedules around our heartfelt desires? The process should be done with rational intentionality. One key to remember is this: nothing gets done that does not get into your schedule. In the end, only those things we are willing to put time into get done. We have enough time to be successful. It is by choice we invest our 168 hours a week. There is enough time for you to accomplish your life vision. Your time is your life.

If we keep our vision clearly in front of us and do not waver in our intention for healthy change, these methods can take us from where we are living to where we want to live. Here is an overview of how to make this process applicable to your real life:

1. Write your current schedule on a chart. Make this large enough so you can clearly see it and work with it. Highlight the hours you have activities not consistent with your life vision. List on the chart the level of commitment you have to this inconsistent activity.

2. Now, write an ideal schedule with what you consider to be "unchangeable current realities", such as the job you currently have. If your job is within your life vision statement, then that makes it easier. But if not, recognize big changes will take time and planning. Right now, we are seeing what you could change within your life that would align with your life vision. Put into this ideal schedule all or most of those "consistent" actions you just don't have time to do. If there are some left off, make a separate list of these vision enhancing actions and also list on a scale from one to ten your evaluation of their importance.

3. After you have done this, compare the two charts. Look for places where you can easily take out an activity you have limited commitment to with an activity that would be vision consistent. Right now, you are making suggested changes on

paper so you can see what steps you might want to take.

4. Make a list of all obstacles that exist which will keep you from making your ideal schedule your real schedule. After listing all of these obstacles, develop ideas and plans on how to overcome them.

5. Over the next 90 days attempt to make one change a week where you are intentionally putting in more and more vision enhancing activities and taking out those inconsistent with your vision.

My Current Schedule

	Sunday	Monday	Tuesday	Wednesday	Thursday	Friday	Saturday
6 AM							
7 AM							
8 AM							
9 AM							
10 AM							
11 AM							
NOON							
1 PM							
2 PM							
3 PM							
4 PM							
5 PM							
6 PM							
7 PM							
8 PM							
9 PM							
10 PM							
11 PM							
12 PM							

My Ideal Schedule

	Sunday	Monday	Tuesday	Wednesday	Thursday	Friday	Saturday
6 AM							
7 AM							
8 AM							
9 AM							
10 AM							
11 AM							
NOON							
1 PM							
2 PM							
3 PM							
4 PM							
5 PM							
6 PM							
7 PM							
8 PM							
9 PM							
10 PM							
11 PM							
12 PM							

Vision Enhancing Activities I don't have time to do

1.

2.

3.

4.

5

6.

7.

Obstacles to make my time more vision enhancing	Ways to overcome these obstacles

If this process is applied, within 90 days your schedule will be lived with priorities consistent with your life vision. To the degree this is accomplished, you have gained control of your life and are in the process of succeeding at life.

Your time use will reflect a sane investment of your precious life moments into the most significant activities you can do.

STABLE DEVELOPMENT

To be stable in keeping our life on course, we must be able to set boundaries over our schedule when people attempt to push their agendas into our time. If we do not carefully guard our schedules, then we will be living someone else's schedule. To keep our lives on track will require constant diligence and care. But, if we keep our life vision clearly in front of us, we can keep from losing our vision priority.

One way we can handle some of this pressure in a graceful and giving way, is to "tithe" our time to help others. This can be part of our vision when we decide to give our "gift of time" helping others reach their goals. We need to carefully think through how much time we can realistically give in this manner. This can give us great satisfaction since people are not "taking" our time, but we are consciously "giving" our time as a gift.

Another obstacle we may face is we might not know how to set goals in order to meet the objectives toward reaching our vision. We must first define where the gaps are between our current performances and where we want to be. We can list these in a chart.

Use the following one to get started:

Where I am now	Obstacles	Overcoming Strategies	Positive Actions	Where I want to be
My office is disorganized	I don't have time to organize	I could schedule an "organizing meeting" with myself and face how much time my lack of organization	Get a book on how to organize an office and plan my organization before I actually do it. Envision a well	Having an organized office

99

		cost me.	planned office	
I am impatient	I always feel rushed and this leads to my impatience	Learn to plan and pace your day	Do self talk that reminds you things take longer than planned	Being patient
Where I am now	Obstacles	Overcoming Strategies	Positive Actions	Where I want to be

We should look at our life vision and list every area where we see a gap between who we are and who we want to become. This list should include highly significant things as well as small things. We then need to list the obstacles, plan strategies to overcome the obstacles, and develop ideas of how to move ourselves from where we are to where we want to be. Part of our plan may be to get some professional help in this process. As mentioned, getting the help of mentors, life coaches, and spiritual directors can greatly increase our effectiveness in defining our goals and begin succeeding at life.

Well thought out written goals have a much higher rate of success than generalized whims we rarely think about[19]. When our written goals have an accountability structure, we get feedback on our progress by the actual number of times we reach our goals and this encourages us to accomplish our goals. One of the keys to finding the right methods is seeking people who were once where we are today and are now doing better. Find out what worked for them. We don't have to recreate "fire" if we are humble enough to ask someone for a spark from their fire.

There are also some helpful methods of life management that can come solve many problems. Consider these simple proverbs of effective living:

➢ Always plan twice the time you think a job will take to get done. You can always push some other project ahead of schedule if you finish "early."

➢ It is alright to schedule meetings with yourself. In our society no one questions the importance of having a meeting. So plan to have some quality time with yourself and do activities that enhance your vision.

➢ Schedule a block of time to answer phone calls and e-mails. Also, schedule phone calls so you do not have to play phone tag.

---

[19] While there are myths of studies done at Yale and Harvard proving the effectiveness of written goals there has been an actual study done which does demonstrate that written goals work. http://sidsavara.com/wp-content/uploads/2008/09/researchsummary2.pdf

➢ Plan a mental health day once a quarter. Just plan a day to think and journal. Check to see if your direction is still moving in the direction of your dreams. The world will not end if you take time to unwind and think.

➢ Begin each day reading significant literature that inspires you. This should include the Bible. Take time to write down insights in a journal. Give yourself thirty minutes a day for prayer, reflection, reading, and meditation. You will be amazed how this enhances your life and improves your decisions.

➢ Schedule time for regular exercise. This should be fun and relaxing, not intimidating. Do something simple you enjoy regularly. It will reduce your stress and help you be more effective.

➢ Take a ten minute break every two hours you work. Don't skip lunch. Don't treat yourself worse than you would an employee. Work at a consistent rate and don't live in panic.

➢ Take time with your children you wish your parents had taken to be with you.

➢ Remember that relationships should last longer than jobs. Check your values and make sure the people you love know they are important.

➢ Relationships have to be given a lot of time to be healthy. When we attempt to become efficient in our relationships, they fail. The great moments of our relationships come at the most unexpected times. Give them time.

➢ Plan to "spoil" yourself. Put fun, laughter, and joy into your planned use of time

➢ Plan to give to a cause that you have a passion for and believe will make a difference in the world. To succeed at life we have to leave a legacy of good deeds.

If we stop living in panic and start living in the plan, then we will see our stress levels decrease and our satisfaction increase.

Keep your life vision in front of you. Recommit your strong intention daily to see it become a reality. Seek out the best methods and put them into your schedule. Be consistent and focused while giving yourself time to relax, reflect, and enjoy. Life is a marathon, so once we get our direction right, time is our friend. It is direction, not perfection that matters.

SPIRITUAL INFLUENCES

The account of creation found in the first chapter of Genesis is a source of great controversy in our society. However, it is a wonderful source of inspiration when thinking through a plan to accomplish our life vision. God had a vision to create His Kingdom paradise on earth. He did this in "six days." His intention was set and His methods were powerful. In the creation plan, God gave us an example of how we also can create. [20]

As we look at Genesis we notice it is a well structured and thought provoking piece of literature. It reflects a well planned creation. As we get beyond the surface of the text, we find the following structure:

Day One: God created the Light	**Day Four:** God created the sun, moon, and stars
Day Two: God created the sky and sea	**Day Five:** God created the creatures in the sky and sea
Day Three: God created the land and vegetation	**Day Six:** God created the animals and man who would populate the land and eat the vegetation
Day Seven: A day to enjoy what had been made and rest in that joy	

From this account, we learn the following about planning and time management:

---

[20] For an approach to reconciling science and faith see; *Intelligent Design: The Bridge Between Science & Theology* by William A. Dembski and *Genesis and the Big Bang: The Discovery Of Harmony Between Modern Science And The Bible* by Gerald Schroeder

➤ God did not try to do everything at once even though He could have done it that way. He is a God of historical process. If gradual process is good enough for God, it should be good enough for us.

➤ God had logically thought through His creation. The parts and the whole of creation line up. There is a structure and harmony to what He does. This would indicate we should also seek to be logical and systematic in how we plan the life vision He has called us to create

➤ God moved from the large to the small. First He set up the cosmic universe and then He created the flowers. This helps us as well.

➤ God's creation was done to provide a healthy environment for relationships between men and women. God's motive ultimately is love, as God is love. It should also be a key element in all of our planning.

➤ There is a time to work and a time to rest. We are called to work hard but also to rest. Our plan needs to include rest, renewal, reflection, and recreation.

Made in the image of God, we are called to reflect God in our work. He has given us our life vision and calling. It is for our good and the good of mankind, and for His glory to accomplish it. Therefore, let us seek to understand the particular will of God for our lives and do it with all our heart. Ultimately, this goal is what succeeding at life is all about.

Summary

A clear life vision will be empowered when we make a decision to weave it into the fabric of our life and schedules. Only when we commit our time have we made a true commitment. By progressively subtracting from our lives those things that hinder our vision and adding into our lives those actions that nurture our life vision, we will find our direction to bring our inner and outer worlds into harmony. This is what it takes to succeed at life.

Thoughts

Chapter Five Exercises

1. Review the entire process you have learned in this book. Where has that process broken down in your application? What could be done to get this process working for you?

2. How many changes must you make to move from your real to your ideal schedule? If you made one change a week, how long would this take you? Would it be worth it to go through the pain of progressive change? Why or why not? What could you do to make the changes easier?

3. What do you see as the greatest obstacles to you living out your life vision? Who could you talk to about how to remove them?

Journal for Chapter Five

What thoughts and feelings are you having after reading this

chapter?

_____

_____

_____

_____

_____

_____

_____

_____

_____

_____

_____

_____

_____

_____

_____

_____

_____

_____

_____

_____

_____

_____

In the end we must choose whether we scoff and mock the positive and good or we decide to embrace vision, intention, and wise process. To succeed at life is our decision.

Final Word – How To Make This Matter

You have honored me by taking this journey with me. I hope and pray you have found help for your heart in this journey. We were not seeking information but transformation.

Transformation is not easy. Insanity comes easier to many of us than sanity. Dysfunction is practiced without proper training. One of the practical implications of the second law of thermodynamics is there always is a constant reduction in the amount of effective power we have to use. The world is in a sinful state and no longer a paradise. Therefore, success only comes when we carefully plan for it.

But thank God, He has not given up on us or on our world. It is also critical we do not give up either. He is so committed to His creation. He sent Jesus to die for our sins and be raised to glory. We must be convinced there remains a divine plan for our existence we can discover and accomplish through our life vision.

For the guidance in this book to matter, you must decide the encouragement given to you for personal change has more potency than all the voices saying you cannot change. Ultimately, the success or failure of what you have received lies in your hands. All those who have applied these principles are in the process of succeeding at life. Most of those who heard them and did not apply these principles are just where they were before they heard or are in even worse shape. Somehow, when we don't decide we actually do decide. So let me remind you of something I told you in the beginning.

Why choose to believe?

Because:

All unbelief offers

Is what you have now

Is what you have had in the past

Anger at not having answers

Bitterness over the loss of wholeness

Despair over never being whole

And Because:

Belief offers

A future better than today

An answer to the frustration of the past

Joy in finding answers

Peace in the experience of increasing wholeness

Purpose in beginning to reflect our healthy whole selves

How can you make all we have processed together matter? You must believe and act consistently with that faith. If you do that, you have started the journey towards succeeding at life. May the God of grace, allow you to have such faith today. Shalom (peace) be with you.

MY FINAL JOURNAL
What should I apply from this book into my life?

MY FINAL JOURNAL

What should I apply from this book into my life?

_____

_____

_____

_____

_____

_____

_____

_____

_____

_____

_____

_____

_____

_____

_____

_____

_____

MY FINAL JOURNAL

What should I apply from this book into my life?

MY FINAL JOURNAL

What should I apply from this book into my life?

_____

_____

_____

_____

_____

_____

_____

_____

_____

_____

_____

_____

_____

_____

_____

_____

_____

_____

MY FINAL JOURNAL
What should I apply from this book into my life?

_____

_____

_____

_____

_____

_____

_____

_____

_____

_____

_____

_____

_____

_____

_____

_____

_____

_____

MY FINAL JOURNAL
What should I apply from this book into my life?

MY FINAL JOURNAL

What should I apply from this book into my life?

_____

_____

_____

_____

_____

_____

_____

_____

_____

_____

_____

_____

_____

_____

_____

_____

_____

_____

MY FINAL JOURNAL
What should I apply from this book into my life?

MY FINAL JOURNAL
What should I apply from this book into my life?

_____

_____

_____

_____

_____

_____

_____

_____

_____

_____

_____

_____

_____

_____

_____

_____

_____

_____

MY FINAL JOURNAL

What should I apply from this book into my life?

_____

_____

_____

_____

_____

_____

_____

_____

_____

_____

_____

_____

_____

_____

_____

_____

_____

MY FINAL JOURNAL
What should I apply from this book into my life?

_____

_____

_____

_____

_____

_____

_____

_____

_____

_____

_____

_____

_____

_____

_____

_____

_____

_____

_____

_____

MY FINAL JOURNAL

What should I apply from this book into my life?

_____

_____

_____

_____

_____

_____

_____

_____

_____

_____

_____

_____

_____

_____

_____

_____

An Appendix On Matters of Faith

I appreciate and respect those of you who are reading this book, but do not share my Christian faith. I believe that we can gain insight from people even when we do not agree with their worldview. This is true tolerance.

Tolerance is not pretending we all agree or silencing discussion of significant issues in the world, but rather recognizing the differences as real and significant, and treating each other with respect in the midst of our talking about ideas. Such a view of tolerance could help us better understand each other. Those of you who have read this book and are not coming from a Christian worldview have demonstrated tolerance and I am honored.

What do I believe about faith? I believe a person's faith is their worldview. I think this worldview or philosophy should be reasonable and rational. It should be open to intelligent debate and related to facts. I believe a worldview should attempt to understand and define what really is.

One of the problems in our society is that while allowing people different views of the world, the impression is given that all views of the world are equally believable. This clearly is not the case. A worldview that says the earth is flat is not as believable as one that says the world is a sphere and orbits the sun. Because of the facts we have discovered about reality through scientific research understanding the earth as sphere is a radically better understanding of reality than the flat earth view.

As a person of Christian faith, this means that I believe with intellectual integrity the Christian worldview is the best understanding of reality and is the truth of why things exist. This type of intellectual faith requires study, reflection, and dialogue. Some books that I think can help in understanding the intellectual case for Christianity are:

- *An Introduction to Christian Apologetics: A Philosophic Defense of the Trinitarian-Theistic Faith* by Edward John Carnell
- *The Problem of Pain* by C. S. Lewis
- *Miracles* by C. S. Lewis
- *The Universe Next Door: A Basic Worldview Catalog*, 5th Edition by James W. Sire
- *How to Think About God: A Guide for the 20th-Century Pagan* by Mortimer Jerome Adler

It is important that we have a strong faith in our view of the world. The world will be changed by "true believers". Without a strong intellectual conviction in a "faith" system of belief, we will lack the passion and purpose necessary to change our lives. [21]

However, having "intellectual faith" in the Christian worldview is not sufficient. This would be a "cultural Christian" but such faith would fall eighteen inches short of being a "true believer" in Christ. (Eighteen inches is the distance from the head to the heart.) In addition to this intellectual commitment to Christianity as a world and life view, one must personally commit to the person of Messiah Jesus as the unique incarnation of deity and trust Him on a personal level. He is my ultimate source of truth, the forgiver of my sins through His death on the cross, and has the ultimate authority in my life. Jesus is my divine Hero, Leader, Savior, Hope, and Boss. I made a personal and sincere pledge of loyalty to Jesus to be His follower in this world. Only then was I a "true believer". Even here we must think about direction and not perfection. A commitment to Jesus at this personal level will not be perfect, but it must be sincere and growing.

Finally, this faith in the person of Jesus Christ must translate into a practical trust of Jesus watching over us and being involved in our daily lives. This means we must exercise our faith in daily prayer, work, attitudes, and decisions. Our trust in Jesus must transpose into our daily lifestyle. To do this we must develop spiritual disciplines. Some books that can help in developing spiritual disciplines are:

- *Celebration of Discipline: The Path to Spiritual Growth* by Richard Foster
- *Spiritual Classics : Selected Readings for Individuals and Groups on the Twelve Spiritual Disciplines* by Richard J. Foster, Emilie Griffin, and Renovare
- *The Spirit of the Disciplines: Understanding How God Changes Lives* by Dallas Willard and Richard Foster

---

[21] Lee Strobel, *The Case for Christ: A Journalist's Personal Investigation of the Evidence for Jesus,* (Grand Rapids, Michigan: Zondervan, 1998) and William Hasker and C. Stephen Evans, *Metaphysics: Constructing a Worldview (Contours of Christian Philosophy* (Downers Grove, Illinois: InterVarsity Press, 1983)

- *Spiritual Disciplines for the Christian Life* by Donald S. Whitney

    I do believe people should have Christian faith. I think it moves us towards accepting reality. It allows us not only to succeed at life now, but forever. If you have questions about Christian faith please contact me at: normwise@bellsouth.net. I hope you will think consider how faith can help you succeed at life.

Notes

_____

_____

_____

_____

_____

_____

_____

_____

_____

GLOSSARY

Proactive – The belief we are able to respond to life and take practical actions to improve our state of being. To be proactive is to take 100% responsibility for one's thoughts, actions, words, moods, and emotions. Proactive people show a willingness to confess their wrong and feel able to strive to correct it by doing right. This outlook rejects the idea that our thoughts, words, actions, moods, and emotions are normally involuntary responses caused by people or genetics.

Sanity – To see reality as it really is and desire to adapt appropriately

Stability – To have the strength, skill, and perseverance to maintain sanity when circumstances change.

Spirituality – Spirituality at the lowest level is to adapt to the eternal principles governing reality and live by them. (For the author spirituality is much more than this since it includes an understanding of having a personal union and communion with the living God through the person of Jesus the Messiah. The topic of spirituality is clearly an area of great controversy and disagreement. Yet, while filled with controversy and emotion, spirituality is a vital area for us to process and develop to become whole. Part of becoming a fully functioning adult is processing the area of spirituality and developing a set of values that will govern and guide us The author is a conservative evangelical Christian. Every effort will be made to encourage the reader to think about their own spirituality without thinking for a moment that it will be exactly like that of the author. However, it is important for every person to seriously address the ultimate questions of life and determine as "proactive" adults what spiritual reality is and adapt to it.)

Helpful Tool To Improve Effectiveness

ThinkTQ.com

I found something in which I thought you would be interested. I am excited about it so I am sharing it with everyone who reads my book.

This company (ThinkTQ.com) has developed a new training system that helps people achieve their goals sooner (personally and professionally) -- by giving you the tools to immediately produce better results. Their starter package costs nothing but 2 minutes of your time.

They are the ONLY people I know of in the world who can quickly show you...

   * What you are doing RIGHT -- so you can do MORE of that...

   * What you are doing WRONG -- so you can do LESS of that...

   * Exactly what you need to do DIFFERENT to accelerate your success.

To introduce their new product line, they are giving away 10 million audio CD training programs covering different areas of your performance: setting goals, making plans, team-building,

organization, time management, your attitude, etc.

You should get one before they run out! There's no obligation

to purchase anything.

The idea is to simply choose one area of your performance,

either a major strength... and make it stronger... or a limiting

weakness... and eliminate it. Either way, this program focuses

on personal improvement in a whole new way.

They have all kinds of simple on-line tests, assessments,

workshops and "Daily Lessons in Excellence" email training

program that really is encouraging! I highly recommend it.

To sign up, just go to http://www.ThinkTQ.com/Gift

Enter this number in the Gift Certificate box: 110173

(this is how I get credit!)

May this help you in your search for success!

26411720R00076

Made in the USA
Charleston, SC
06 February 2014